GREEKTOWN CHICAGO

ITS HISTORY - ITS RECIPES

BY ALEXA GANAKOS

INTRODUCTION BY
HARRY MARK PETRAKIS

COLOR PHOTOGRAPHY BY
KATHERINE BISH

G. BRADLEY PUBLISHING, INC. • ST. LOUIS, MISSOURI 63131

PUBLICATION STAFF

Author.......................................Alexa Elaine Ganakos

Food Editor................................Maria Fotinopoulos

Copy Editor ....Gloria Baraks

Production Coordinator..............Christopher Ganos

Color Photography ....Katherine Bish

Book Design ....Diane Kramer

Photo Design ....Michael Bruner

Cover Jacket Design ....Michael Bruner

Publisher ....G. Bradley Publishing, Inc.

Sponsor........Hellenic Museum and Cultural Center

DEDICATION

A graduate of Eastern Illinois University School of Journalism, Katherine Bish has been telling stories through pictures since 1998. Her food photography has appeared in *St. Louis Magazine, Sauce Magazine,* and *St. Louis Post-Dispatch.* Her work has also been featured in *National Geographic Traveler* and *Food and Wine.*

ISBN 0-9774512-0-8
Printed in the U.S.A.

Please check the G. Bradley Publishing website to review other Midwest history books such as this:
www.gbradleypublishing.com

TABLE OF CONTENTS

MEMORIES OF BEING GREEK BY HARRY MARK PETRAKIS

The neighborhood on the South Side of Chicago that encircled my father's parish in the period of the 1930s and 1940s, might have been villages transplanted from Greece into America. Many of the apartments in the dingy brick two-story and three-story buildings along our street were occupied by immigrants. There were not only Greeks but Italians and Serbs as well as Polish and German Jewish refugees fleeing the Nazis and the war in Europe. The hallways of our building smelled of the dishes of a half-dozen countries. From the hidden back porches on summer nights, a medley of tongues spiraled into the darkness.

The life of our Greek community centered about the church in which my family played a pivotal role because my father was the priest. Early Sunday mornings, with the first tracings of dawn glimmering over the rooftops of buildings, I'd walk beside my father on our way to church. The shops we passed were shuttered and shadowed, the only other sign of life–a prowling tomcat returning from some midnight revel.

We'd enter the dark silent church, damp with the coolness of the night. Our sexton, Mr. Spiro, would begin lighting the candles before the stern-visaged icons of the saints. The church would come slowly into warmth and light.

I'd help my father don his vestments and then joined the other altar boys. All

Members of the Petrakis family, circa 1934, from left to right: Tasula, Reverend Mark Petrakis, Dan, Irene, Harry, seated; Manuel, Barbara, and Presbytera Petrakis. Rev. Petrakis and members of his family first came to the United States in 1916 from Crete and served the coal mining community of Carbon County, Utah, before finally ending up in Chicago in 1923 to lead the parish of Sts. Constantine & Helen Greek Orthodox Church. Reverend Petrakis died in 1951. Presbytera founded many philanthropic organizations and remained active in them until her death in 1979 at the age of 91. Son Harry Mark Petrakis is the author of 20 books. He intertwines stories of the Greek immigrant experience in much of his writings.

this time the church was filling with people. The girls of the choir, dark-haired nymphs clad in their black robes with white collars would assemble in the choir loft under the direction of the handsome, sonorous-voiced choirmaster, Mr. George. When my father emerged from the sanctuary to begin the service, the candles glowing like specks of flame on his vestments, I felt the awesome power of the moment, for in addition to being spiritual father to all the parish, he was blood-father to me.

All through what seemed to me at the time to be an interminable liturgy, we altar boys emerged and retreated from the sanctuary, holding our long candlesticks. Our final duty was to hold the baskets of *andethero* the tiny pieces of sanctified bread my father dispensed to each parishioner that passed.

At the end of the service, we exited the church into a clamorous throng of people buoyantly greeting one another. Moving briskly among them would be the harsh-voiced crier who had driven up on his motorcycle to hawk Greek newspapers. There was also an apron-clad vendor selling the round, sesame-sprinkled *kouloures*. If there had been a memorial service for someone deceased, there would also be small plastic bags containing the savory currant and powder-sugared *sitari*, the boiled wheat used to memorialize the dead.

Each Sunday after church our family, along with several visitors, gathered in our dining room for lunch in which my mother replicated the miracle of the loaves and fishes. She met the contingencies of the depression by preparing large pans of *pilaf*–the appetizing, white kerneled rice often served with a tangy tomato sauce. Into this concoction my mother inserted one scrawny chicken carved so artfully one thought the pilaf contained at least three of the hapless fowl.

My father sat at the head of our table, my mother at the foot. Arrayed along the sides were my brothers and sisters ranging in age from eight to twenty-five. In addition there were usually several visitors my father or mother had invited to join us for lunch.

For years I could not comprehend why, with barely enough food to adequately feed our own family, my parents felt compelled to invite strangers for lunch. Later in my life I finally understood when I read a story in one of the books of Nikos Kazantzakis written while he was traveling in Greece. Stopping in a village for the night, he knocked on the door of the small house adjoining the church which he took to be the rectory. The village priest answered and when Kazantzakis asked for shelter for the night, the priest offered him a bowl of soup and some cheese and bread and then took him to a room where he spent the night.

Kazantzakis didn't learn until after he had left the house in the morning that the priest had lost his son in an accident two days before. While Kazantzakis slept, in another room of the house, the priest's dead son was being waked. But *filoxenia* decreed that he could not be turned away.

To the Greeks, *filoxenia* or hospitality, is almost a religion. The same root word, *filo* or friend, is added to the Greek word *xeno,* or stranger, indicating that Greeks did not differentiate between the way one treated a friend and the way one treated a stranger.

The most important religious holiday of our year was Easter. We prepared for Holy Week by fasting for forty days. My father fasted most stringently, and by the end of the forty days had become pale-cheeked and weary. The rest of us were not as diligent but by the end were still famished. One of the calamities of my childhood came during such a fast when on the day I was to receive holy communion I inadvertently swallowed a piece of banana. As we knelt in a line of parishioners before the altar, my father bent to dispense communion, my mother whispered to him my misdemeanor. My father somberly refused me communion. I still recall the shocked faces of the parishioners as I retreated from the altar, their expressions registering horror as they contemplated the crimes of murder, pillage, and arson, for which

I had been rejected by my own father. In my anguish I wanted to cry out to them that my only crime involved a paltry bite of a banana.

The conclusion of Holy Week was the night of *Anastasis* when at midnight the church would be plunged into darkness. Then a solitary candle was lit and from that candle, hundreds of other candles were kindled so they gleamed like stars in the velvet night.

Christos Anesti! "Christ is Risen!" We almost sang the words. *Alithos Anesti!* "Truly He is risen!" was the response.

And in that moment we felt redeemed and sanctified ourselves, our souls purified, in the ancient ritual of resurrection.

Afterwards we'd go home to the paschal feast, *mageritsa*, lamb, browned potatoes, at the end cracking the blood red eggs. Finally, collapsing into bed, for the first time our hunger really sated, to sleep comforted by the presence of parents and brothers and sisters, existing like sentries in the watchfires of our night.

Many years have passed since those garlanded Easters of my childhood. My parents are dead now, lying side by side under patches of cemetery sod as are most of my sisters and brothers. But even with the passing of decades, that warm, cloistered world of our parents and grandparents remains vivid to me to this day. Every church service, wedding, baptism, festival we attend and celebrate now is haunted by the ghosts of those who came before us, strangers into a strange, often hostile land, struggling to make a place for themselves and for those generations that followed.

FOREWORD

While the historic significance of Greece from its glorious ancient days remains unparalleled throughout the centuries, the stories of the Greek immigrant experience are familiar and cross-cultural. With certainty, the Greek immigrants who settled in America loved their new country and gave back to it, defended it, and are responsible for the new generation that must prepare the next that waits to receive the torch.

The Hellenic Museum and Cultural Center is privileged to support historic preservation as it strives to feature and honor what is at the core of its mission – *Αγαπε* (love), *Ελπιδα* (hope) and *Γενεεσ* (generations).

The mission of the Hellenic Museum and Cultural Center extends beyond capturing the past, however. It is also about the present experience; encouraging responsibility and compassion among its citizens, embracing the stranger, and celebrating with the PhilHellene (friend) through arts and education.

As part of the Greek culture well-known for providing a lively, engaging, and family-like experience, the national Hellenic Museum and Cultural Center is pleased to find its home in Chicago's Greektown and embraces its visitors with a warm and inviting welcome.

Greektown Chicago: Its History, Its Recipes is a uniquely creative blend of this past, the present, and, most decidedly, the delicious.

Like art, music, drama, and dance–cuisine is yet another wonderful way in which individuals interpret and experience a culture. With conversation flowing and spirits rising, we have all found ourselves immersed before simple meals or wonderful banquets that represent the true Greek experience. This publication features several fine Greek restaurants which have opened their doors and kitchens to give the reader a flavor of the best of Greek cuisine.

We look forward to seeing you in Chicago's Greektown!

Elaine Kollintzas Drikakis
Executive Director

The staff at the Hellenic Museum and Cultural Center. Left to right, standing, Antonia Callas, Allison Heller Fluecke, Maria Constantinides; seated, Janine Weiss, Elaine Kollintzas Drikakis.

HELLENIC MUSEUM
AND CULTURAL CENTER
A National Institution

Mission

To be the nation's foremost center
of Hellenic history, culture, and the arts,
where the public can explore the legacy of the
Greek immigrant experience in America
and examine the influence of Hellenic
culture and people from antiquity to the present.

"We always thought of ourselves as Greeks in America, because from the time we were young people, we were always told we were going to go back."

REGISTRATION CERTIFICATE.

To whom it may concern, Greetings: No. 68

THESE PRESENTS ATTEST.   (This number must correspond with that on the Registration Card.)

That in accordance with the proclamation of the President of the United States, and in compliance with law,

George L. Thomas Bloomington
(Name)   (City or P.O.)

Precinct 14 County of McLean, State of Illinois

has submitted himself to registration and has by me been duly registered this 5th

day of June, 1917

D. Max Haughey
Registrar.

Documentation was always an important part of the immigrant experience.

The Zaganos family immigrated to America in 1907. Helen, Evangelos, Olga, and Samuel Evangelos are shown in this 1920 photo.

After immigrating to Chicago and raising a family with Thomas Mallers, Helen Haralambapoulos Mallers is pictured in 1918 with her five sons; Anthony, Nicholas, Thomas, Louis, and Theodore after she was widowed. She later married Thomas Kanakis.

COMING TO AMERICA

Greeks began their trek to Chicago, and for a larger part to America, possibly as early as 1492 with the voyage of Columbus. It was well known that Greeks were experienced and adventuresome sailors, so many early explorers and merchants traveled to Greece to recruit a Greek crew. In 1767, immigration to the United States picked up with a large Greek colony forming on Florida's Atlantic coast at New Smyrna. Once immigrants arrived in the United States, the Mississipppi River served as an important waterway to help transport Greeks up to Chicago in the 1840s where many became traders at Fort Dearborn.

Even with the elusive promise of a better life in America, the journey from Greece was not an easy one. However, after enduring severe hardships in Greece, Greeks were ready for a new beginning. In Greece, after 1890 the economy was in the final stages of collapse. Crop and soil conditions had deteriorated and property costs continued to rise. In addition, there was little employment, and the pressure for providing enough money for a daughter's dowry and paying off debts were formidable issues that faced Greeks.

Amongst the poverty and political turmoil, which stemmed from Turkish control, as well as a civil war, many men rose to the challenge of finding new opportunities in America. They left

Boats departing from the port of Patras, Greece to catch a steamship coming to America in 1910.

their families behind, promising them a better life when they returned with money earned from their success in America. According to research by Greek-American historian Andrew Kopan, Ph.D., one of these early pioneers to settle in Chicago was Captain Nicholas Peppas who arrived in 1857 and made his home on Kinzie Street for more than 50 years. Then in 1869, the first Greek-American child was born in the city, Frank Combiths. Interestingly enough, Frank did not have a Greek mother, because at the time, more men were making the immigrant journey than women.

News of America's riches traveled

fast especially through the efforts of Christ Chakonas who was considered the "Columbus of Sparta." When Chakonas came to Chicago in 1872, he recognized the need for permanent laborers to rebuild the city after the Great Fire of 1871. Chakonas returned to Sparta and informed his neighbors of the golden opportunities. Many Spartans made the long journey to America and became Chicagoans. Once Spartan success stories reached neighboring villages in Greece, many from the Laconia and Arcadian regions also made the voyage to the United States, and ultimately Chicago.

In 1885, the first reported Greek woman to arrive in Chicago was Mrs. Peter Pooley, nee Bitzis, the wife of a sea captain from the island of Corfu. In the early years of immigration, it was specu-

The damage done by the Chicago Fire in 1871 provided opportunities for Greeks to come to America to help rebuild the city.

lated that nine of every ten Greeks were male. With the arrival of more Greek women in America, more societies and churches formed, thus recreating some of their communal village experiences from Greece.

With the United States serving as a new home for immigrants escaping troubles in Europe, the Bureau of Immigration formed in 1890. The immigration station opened in 1892 on New York's famed Ellis Island. Many Greeks from the Peloponnesus came through this station in the 1890s. The economic catalyst was the price of one of the peninsula's main crops, currants, which

had dropped drastically. In addition, the great steamships debuting in the early 20th century provided a larger-scale operation to transport dreamers from Europe to America. A three-month trip was now down to two to three weeks.

Most Greeks left for their journey from port cities like Patras or Pireaus. Many times they were routed around different ports in the Mediterranean before heading steadfastly to America. One Greek notes, "My sister left for

America two weeks before my younger brother and I. When we boarded the steamship bound for America, we saw a familiar face–my sister's! After my sister originally boarded weeks earlier, the ship stopped to pick up other passengers and circled back to our port for a second time before heading to America."

Because most Greeks had little money, and sold what they had in order to afford a ticket to America, they traveled in steerage, which was located at the bottom of the boat and marked by cramped conditions. There were sepa-

Peter and Georgia Pooley emigrated from Corfu, Greece in 1885.

George Brown (Kotakis) was one of the first Greek immigrants to arrive in Chicago. Originally from the island of Samos, he came to Chicago in 1859 by way of New Orleans. He served in the Union Army during the Civil War. Upon his return to Chicago, he became a barber and operated a shop in the Loop for many years. He is photographed with his family, circa 1877.

In 1885 Mrs. Georgia Bitzis Pooley was one of the first Greek women to come to Chicago from Corfu, Greece. Mrs. Pooley was well-educated with strong organizational skills. These attributes helped her serve as the beacon in the forming Greek community. She guided many of the young Greek men to live morally and commit to a church community. Alongside the Slavic-Orthodox church communities, she organized the Greco-Slavic Brotherhood to help form the first common house of Orthodox worship in Chicago.

rate dormitories for single men, single women, and families–and there was little privacy. Beds were tightly packed, sometimes stacked in three-tiered bunks. The smell of human existence and unbathed bodies filled the air. There was little food to eat; mostly soup, potatoes, and fish, or whatever the immigrant brought with him, and many times, it was spoiled. Diseases abounded, as well as head lice. Along with sea-sickness, it was enough to make the immigrant wonder why he had left his homeland. By 1910, many of the steerage sections were replaced with third-class cabins which held four to six people, and meals were handed out on deck in tin mess kits or served in basic dining rooms.

The Statue of Liberty was a welcome sight after the arduous trip. Between the years of 1900-1920, 351,720 Greeks immigrated to the United States. They were warmly greeted by the statue of a lady who resembled a torchbearer from the Greek Olympic games. With her one arm raised confidently, and her other arm clutching a tablet, she symbolized a Hellene clenching onto his identity to pass on to future generations.

When disembarking at the Hudson River piers, third-class or steerage travelers were shuffled onto open-air ferry boats, which were freezing in the winter, and stifling hot in the summer, and transfered across the harbor to Ellis Island. Because the harbor could be filled with steamships, often the new arrivals were held in steerage for days waiting for a ferry. So, just when they thought their journey had ended, the disembarcation and Ellis Island bureaucracy kept them from taking their first steps on American soil.

Once at Ellis Island, a factory-like system was enforced to move immigrants through the inspection process in the Main Hall. Because of the thousands of immigrants from various countries arriving daily, this process took days. Without the immigrant's knowledge, inspectors were scrutinizing the long lines for signs of illness. The examination started as they stood on the dock headed for the Baggage Room or climbed the steep stairs to the Registry Room where they were officially recorded off the steamship manifest. Eagle-eyed inspectors noted all limping, coughing, and other disablities. They also checked for 60 symptoms that indicated tuberculosis, anemia, scalp fun-

"My father came to this country in 1919 and spent 10 years here and became economically independent, believe it or not. He went back to Greece in 1929. While in the U.S., he was supporting four brothers, plus his mother, by sending money back to Greece."

In the same New York port where the Statue of Liberty proudly stands, the vast, sterile rooms at Ellis Island have been converted (since its closing in 1954) to the Ellis Island Immigration Museum. This site commemorates the immigrants' courageous crossing, and their humbling experience as they passed through Ellis Island.

gus–and even insanity. Any suspicious new arrivals were either held in quarantine, in a hospital, or a small percentage were sent back to Greece.

Once in America, Greeks sought out the larger cities to begin their new lives and traveled by railroad to meet already established relatives. New York, Chicago, Detroit, San Francisco, and Lowell, Massachusetts boasted the largest Greek populations in 1920. The urban environment allowed for employment opportunities much different than their failed Greek farming experiences. Furthermore, the ability to find countrymen that spoke their native language was much easier in these urban enclaves.

Because of the success stories of earlier Greek pioneers in Chicago, (a city with roughly the same population as all of Greece at the time), and the opportunity to be part of the rebirth and

industrialization of the city following the Great Fire, immigrants flowed into Chicago. The census reports 245 Greeks in Chicago in 1890. However, in 1900 the number totaled 1,493 and in 1920 it was estimated at 15,000 (a conservative estimate). It is difficult to pinpoint an accurate number of Greeks in Chicago during the first two decades of the 20th century when immigration to the area reached its peak, because many Greek men traveled out West to work on the railroad from April through November and only about a quarter of the Greeks remained in the city during those summer months to be counted.

The first Greek area in Chicago was

Continued on page 15

Posing proudly is the Executive Council of the Hellenic League for the Molding of Young Men in 1910. This league formed in 1908 and gave young men the opportunity to participate in paramilitary and athletic experiences at Hull House under the leadership of former Greek army officers. This training proved beneficial when Greeks (30-40,000 in total from the U.S.) returned home to fight the Balkan War of 1912-1913.

"My mother's niece made the voyage to America with her, leaving her family behind. Upon examination, it was found that one eye was tearing, so the authorities placed a large chalk mark on her clothing. My mother knew what that meant–she would be detained and possibly split apart from the family, or worse yet, denied entry. So, without even a second thought, my mother discreetly wiped the chalk mark off of her neice's back and had her join the family in the rest of the processing, as if nothing had happened."

Following a fanfare of a military band, ceremonies at Hull House, and special blessings given at Holy Trinity Greek Orthodox Church, over 300 men congregated at Union Station in 1912 to return to Greece to help fight in the Balkan Wars. More than 3,000 men left from Chicago, and many returned after the war with wives.

A Hull-House resident told a reporter in 1902, "We knew nothing of them [the Greeks] until one night we observed the street and the saloon above us in Halsted Street were filled with them. They were young men, and had arrived recently in search of work. Gradually they have assimilated with the Italians, with whom they seemed to fraternize." [1]

LEAVING THE HOMELAND

In most cases, leaving Greece translated into an opportunity to make money and get a better education. However, the decision to immigrate was not always an easy one, nor was leaving family and friends. Fortunately, as churches and village fraternities formed in America, the Greeks found a way to maintain ties to their homeland and perpetuate their family bonds.

In the early 1920s, George Thodoropoulos had already immigrated from Greece to earn a living, leaving Margaret and their children, photo above, to follow. Their oldest daughter opted to remain in Greece and marry.

William Kakavas, second from right, captures some final moments with relatives before leaving Rapsomati, Greece, for America in 1951.

"My parents were upset [with me leaving]. I was upset. But they said, 'Make up your mind.' And, I came here to better myself."

Ekaterina Robakis Kouchoukos, the second youngest of seven children, leaves her village, photo right, of Lahanatha in Messinia, to join her two older sisters in Chicago. To remind her of her roots, her cousin took this photo of the sheep she tended, while walking cold and barefoot in the mountains.

"I cried because I knew I would never see my Yiayia again."

By the early 1900s Greeks established themselves in the "Delta" section between Harrison and Polk streets, from Halsted to Blue Island Avenue.

Delta is actually a Greek letter of the alphabet that resembles a triangle, a Δ, as does the section where the Greeks settled.

Another interpretation is of connecting river tributaries, forming a river delta, likewise the Greek immigrants (up to 40,000) surged into this area.

Photo right: In 1951, the construction of the Eisenhower expressway, and later the Kennedy expressway each chopped off large sections of the Greek Delta on the north and east. Neighborhood groups of Greeks, Italians, African-Americans, Mexicans, and Puerto Ricans all banded together and worked closely with neighborhood activist, Florence Scala, to save the area from urban expansion. However, in 1963, the United State Supreme Court brought an end to the Halsted-Harrison litigation and residents, with little compensation, were given notice to move within a year. Urban expansion included building the University of Illinois at Chicago campus and classes began at the new facility in 1965. The historic movie Kali Nihta, Socrates (Good Night, Socrates), *directed and filmed by Northwestern graduate students, captures the death of this residential community as seen through the eyes of a ten-year-old Greek boy.*

Continued from page 12

formed in the 1890s and hovered north of the Loop, near Clark and Kinzie streets. Greek shops and residences gave a sense of permanency to the area, although the mindset of many of these Greeks was one of "repatriation." They knew they would earn enough money and return home. Most of these early Greeks found employment on the railroads, in the stockyards, as laborers rebuilding Chicago, and as peddlers.

Unlike other ethnic groups that may have immigrated to the United States due to religious persecution or for political reasons, Greeks came mostly for economic gain. They were prepared to work hard, send money back to their families, pay off debts, tend to their daughters' dowries (bridal gifts), and

eventually return home.

The geography of Greece itself, with its natural barriers of hillsides, rocky terrain, and islands, all created a strong sense of survival in a village community to become self-sustaining. However, when this was no longer possible in Greece, Greek immigrants brought this spirit to America. And, with the support of their family and "clansmen" from their region they formed tight-knit communities. This sense of belonging and self-sustainment served immigrants well in their new life in the United States. In addition this independence, put many on the path to run their own businesses.

In 1892, Chicago Greeks held the first church service in a rented warehouse located at Randolph and Union streets

near the produce market where most Greeks worked. The first resident priest, Rev. Peter Phiambolis, was named to lead the service. This effort was coordinated through the Lycurgus Society formed by men that had emigrated from Sparta. The church was consecrated on March 25, 1893 at the time of the Columbian Exposition when Bishop Dionysius (Lattas) of Zakynthos, the first hierarch of the Greek Orthodox Church, visited the United States, and specifically, Chicago. This church began in a warehouse, then relocated to 60 East Kinzie, and finally established a permanent home in 1910, located at 1017 North LaSalle at Oak Street. This site became known as the Annunciation Cathedral and serves as the host church for the Metropolitan of

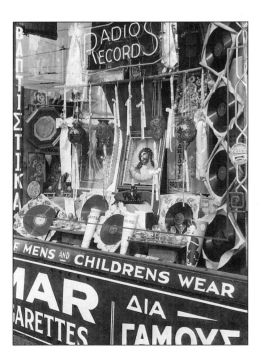

The storefronts of the hustling Greektown neighborhood were reminiscent of the old country yet incorporated the modernity of America, i.e. Coca-Cola and cigarettes. Far left: Mouzakiotis Music Store. Center: the Phoenix Pastry Shop.

The Rt.Rev. Philaretos (Johannides) was the first Greek Orthodox Bishop for the Diocese of Chicago. During the years 1923-1930 in which he served, he led the development of 14 new parishes and catechetical schools to help tutor young Greek Orthodox children with lessons of the faith.

Chicago and the diocese.

Although one would like to imagine all Greeks living and working together in harmony as new immigrants from the same homeland, this was not the case. Because of the longevity and more established group of Greeks congregating near the South Water Street market near Randolph Street, the poorer Greek immigrants, mainly from Arcadia, who started emigrating from the Peloponnesus in 1895, settled in an area on the near west side of the city. This section became known as Greektown or the "Delta" because it resembled the mouth of a river joining other tributaries and these representative thoroughfare branches were Halsted, Harrison, Blue Island, and Polk streets. Today, some of this area is the present location of the University of Illinois at Chicago campus and several major expressways. A few blocks of the physical Hellenic heritage were able to remain on the four-block stretch from Monroe to Van Buren on Halsted Street, the home of the present-day Greektown.

Back at the turn of the century, with the heaviest immigration occurring between 1900-1920, there was much discord amongst the burgeoning Greek communities. The Spartan-based Lycurgus Society and the Tripoli-based Taega Society were two of these early fac-

Greek entrepreneurs took to the streets with open-air wagons selling fresh fruit and vegetables to the growing Chicago population. By the mid-1920s, the wholesale food industry was mainly controlled by the Greeks at the Randolph and South Water Street markets. In addition, they earned their reputation as hard-working businessmen servicing more than 10,000 retail stores in Chicago during this era.

tional groups disagreeing on religious development and other issues. As a result, the Taega society broke off and established Holy Trinity, the first permanent and continuous Greek Orthodox parish in Chicago in 1897 in the Greek Delta. This parish raised funds and purchased the Episcopalian church on Peoria Street. Later, due to urban redevelopment in the area, Holy Trinity relocated to its current location at 6041 West

Diversey Street. Because of this move, a new Greektown soon emerged near Lincoln and West Lawrence Avenue to support the growing Greek population that established homes and businesses in this area.

At one point, there were many Italians living in the Greek Delta who had succeeded the Polish and Irish. The Greeks gradually displaced them, forming the largest and most concentrated Greek community in the United States. And the

intersection of Halsted and Harrison became one of the busiest in the city.

Because of the Delta's slum-like character, humanitarian Jane Addams decided to build her famed Hull House in this section of the 19th Ward of Chicago. Thus she gave immigrants a chance to enjoy enhanced civic and social life as well as educational, athletic, and cultural offerings.

As Chicago was going through a peri-

Greektown was a business center bustling with busy storefronts, food, and fruit peddlers. This peddler pushes his cart past the Kentron Café and Mouzakiotis Music Store.

od of industrialization, more effort was spent erecting new factories than on quality housing. Thus, tenement housing was put up to hold the swelling population. These structures often times had no electricity and only basic plumbing. Extended families lived together and shared limited resources, but always managed to keep a tidy home. In some cases, the newer immigrant was not so lucky.

Upon arriving in Chicago, most Greeks bunked with relatives who had already established a residence and shared one level of a two- or three-story tenement. Since many of these early immigrant

James Lalagos, left, and an employee, standing at the corner of Blue Island and Vernon Park avenues in front of his Acropolis Restaurant and Tavern.

George Damolaris, at left, and his assistant are identified in front of their horse and carriage in 1911. This was the beginning of a successful career in the food vending business for Damolaris.

men either worked on the railroad, or began life on the street as fruit or cart peddlers, they grouped together above horse barns and formed their own version of a family unit.

Their living conditions tended to be dangerously unsanitary. Many single men between 20-30 years old, sometimes slept 15 to a room above an unfinished and dirty barn. Despite the harsh winter-weather conditions or the summer stench from the horses, these determined young men endured almost unbearable living conditions. Earning about $10 a month in the early 1900s, they paid $30 a month communally to stable a

Most of the Greeks who come to the US are from the Peloponnesus. Out of the 424 that lived within a few blocks of Hull House, 205 came from Sparta, 102 from Tripolis, and 5 from Athens. Moreover, most of those who say they came from Sparta and Tripolis had not really lived in those towns but in the country villages nearby. [2]

horse for their peddling business as well as for sleeping accommodations above the barn.

The married men who came over often lived with brothers or cousins or others from their village. As they established more traditional family groups, they were compelled to keep their living conditions clean, comfortable, and orderly. Other unmarried men also shared apartments in a portion of a two- or three-flat building. Sometimes a restaurant or a shoeshine parlor owner whom they worked for owned the building and took in employees as renters with one individual fulfilling the role of boardinghouse cook and caretaker.

OCCUPATIONS OF 956 GREEK MEN IN CHICAGO IN 1909

Laborers	195
Peddlers	178
Waiters and Cooks	105
Owners of Ice Cream Parlors	83
Porters	79
Restaurant-keepers	55
Store-keepers	41
Clerks	31
Fruit Stores	24
Saloon-keepers and Bartenders	15
Candy Stores or Factories	13
Barbers	12
Masons	11
Owners of Shoe Shine Parlors	10
Printers	9
Miscellaneous	89
Not engaged in Gainful Employment	6

"A Study of the Greeks in Chicago" by Grace Abbott, The American Journal of Sociology, Vol XV, No. 3, November 1909

Residents contributed about $4 a week of their $9-12 weekly salaries to receive food and shelter. Sometimes they would not pay anything, but received a reduced salary of $6-$10 because living accommodations were considered part of their wages. In most cases, these conditions were a bit better, as the apartments were furnished and clean, and the men lived comfortably within these non-family groups.

Upon arriving in this new land, many Greeks found themselves working long hours at fruit and vegetable stands, as peddlers, or as bootblacks. Fueled by a dream of setting up their own business, they endured. Even younger, bright-eyed boys came to America, without father or family to serve as apprentices to former fellow villagers who posed as their father or uncle.

Many of these young boys were employed by shoe-shine parlors. In fact, there was an investigation by the United States Bureau of Immigration in 1908 of the shoeshine parlors in the Chicago Loop. The I.P.L., Immigrant Protective League, received several reports of physical abuse to the boys brought over, and also the operation of a padrone system: the boys were treated like slaves and not paid until they repaid their sponsor the cost of transit. The older Greek "patron" would profit, as he received a small reward from the employer for bringing in this new employee. This apprentice system also functioned on the railroads and in coal mining in Utah, where many Greeks worked and eventually rioted.

Clientele at shoe-shine parlors enjoyed receiving service from a Greek who kept to themselves and focused on the job at hand. Moreover, they did not chit-chat with co-workers in their native language, excluding and irking customers.

Despite spending most of their waking hours at work, these immigrant boys saw this as a land of opportunity. They worked between 9 and 16 hours a day, hustling $15-$20 a month, including

continued on page 28

Shoppers admire the fresh lamb sold at Colias Bros. owned by Anthony James Colias and located at the corner of Polk and Halsted streets.

"My grandmother sent my father over here when he was very young. There were other families that took my father in and watched over him. The purpose was to go with his little shoe shine kit, make money, send money back—so then the next brother could come over. And, this is how they did it. Each brother, as they came over, sent money back so she could then have the money to send the rest of the family over. She was the last one to come here."

HULL HOUSE

For Greek Americans, one of the most influential factors in the transition of life in Greece to life in Chicago was the creation of the world-famous social settlement, Hull House in 1889. Established by the passionate Jane Addams, known by many as "The Saint of Halsted Street," Hull House was a second home to Greeks because it was located in the Delta section of the then 19th Ward where many of them resided. The goals of Hull House were to provide a center for higher civic and social life; to initiate and maintain educational and philanthropic enterprises; and to investigate and improve the conditions in the industrial districts in Chicago.

Because of the poor living conditions in the neighborhood, Hull House was a welcome escape from the drudgery of everyday life and the struggles of trying to adapt to a new homeland. This social settlement offered language and vocational classes, athletic programs, the opportunity to perform Greek plays, and meeting rooms to form clubs and host discussions. Because Jane Addams embraced the ideals of the Hellenic culture and encouraged Greeks to be proud of their heritage, Hull House served an important role in unifying Greeks and enhancing their self-image. In fact, the Greeks used Hull House more than any ethnic group and even began to think of it as their own institution.

Jane Addams and Hull House had a tremendous influence on the lives of the early Greek immigrants. In addition to Hull House, she also was instrumental in founding the Immigrant Protective League in 1908 to aid in the process of immigration and Americanization. The staff spoke 12 languages to help its members sort through issues including bringing over family, qualifying for naturalization and citizenship, defending deportation cases, and unfair treatment of immigrants.

"Here on the ash-heap of Chicago was a blossom of something besides success. The house was saturated in the perfume of the stockyards, to make it sweet. A trolley-line ran by its bedroom windows to make it musical. It was thronged with Jews and Greeks and Italians and soulful visitors, to make it restful. It was inhabited by high strung residents to make it easy. But it was the first place in all America where there came to me a sense of the intention of democracy, the first place where I found a flame by which the melting pot melts.....Yet in that strange haven of clear humanitarian faith I discovered what I suppose I had been seeking-the knowledge that America had a soul."

Francis Hackett, an Irish immigrant who came to live at Hull House in 1906 when he was 23 years old.

From 1889 to 1963 Hull House, located at Polk and Halsted streets, served the needs of immigrants in Chicago by providing a physical center for education and socialization.

"And I used to come here every day to school and to learn how to sew…I used to cry; I used to be lonesome. And Miss Jane Addams, God bless her, said, 'Don't cry. This is going to be your new home. Just educate yourself. Start to read.'" [3]

"Numerous lectures and meetings have been held in Bowen Hall during the year in which the speaking was either in Greek or in both Greek and English. On September 19, 1906, a rousing Pan-Hellenic meeting was held to protest against the atrocities at Aghialos. Bowen Hall was quickly filled to its utmost capacity and overflow meetings at the same time were held in the theatre, the gymnasium, the kindergarten room and in every available space of the hallways. The American speakers who attended the meeting will never forget the patriotism burning in the faces of the hundreds of young men in the audience, as they listened to a recital of glories of ancient Greece." [4]

Nobel Peace Prize winner, Jane Addams, was a dedicated Philhellene. On the day of her funeral, shops in Greektown closed and Greeks and other admirers filled the streets in her honor. "They were marching for blocks and blocks all the way around. …there used to be a big yard in the front, it was full with the people. You never saw so many people. Everybody, of all different nationalities. And you could see a lot of tears in the people's eyes. Because she was like a mother to everybody." [9]

Jane Addams is honored by Dr. Nicholas Solas, the Greek Consul General.

"I first talked to Jane Addams early in 1925 or a little before that. She was a great friend of the Greek people since Hull House is situated in what is known as the Greek town in Chicago, around Halsted and Harrison Streets. I was working in that neighborhood for some time as a newspaperman, and I was aware of the tremendous influence Jane Addams had had on the early Greek immigrant. Hull House opened its doors in 1889. There were very few of us here at that time, but Greek immigration started to be felt around Hull House a couple of decades later, after 1907. We had problems, and Jane Addams was always there to straighten them out for us. She was like a mother to us; she was our protector and our advisor. It was a great alliance based on nobility and understanding. What's more, Jane Addams admired Greek culture, and felt that the modern Greeks who had come here to make America their home, possessed many of the virtues of their ancestors." [5]

A welcoming party is hosted at Hull House for newcomers from Greece in 1957.

One of the many groups organized at Hull House was the Greek Educational Association/The Hellenic League for the Molding of Young Men. "In addition to classes in English and mathematics, they formed a corps of cadets, which drilled in three sections, three evenings a week in the rough-house room in the Boys' Club. They claim that military discipline is most useful to those who work in shoe shine parlors and other occupations requiring regular hours."—Hull House Bulletin, 1910.

"A membership of fifty Greek women meets monthly at Hull House, where they discuss cases of need which they have found among their own countrymen. They organized at Hull House with the assistance of Miss Neukom, with whom they have studied the various charitable agencies of Chicago." [6]

The Greek Women Mothers' Club was organized through Hull House and met once a month. The club gave women the chance to talk to each other and helped to ease the transition of coming to America.

"You realize what it is to come from a foreign country. You can't speak the language, you really don't have any relatives, and you can count your friends on one hand. But every little thing that cropped up, Hull House was there to take care of it for you." [7]

Hull House Theater, the first of its kind in the nation, was inaugurated in December 1899 with a presentation of the classical Greek tragedy *The Return of Odysseus*. The actors were Greek immigrants and they attracted wide attention in the city; it was the first public recognition for Greek immigrants in Chicago. The success of *The Return of Odysseus* prompted the Greek community to work on another theatrical production, *Sophocle's Ajax* in December 1903. [8]

"These are real sons of Hellas chanting the songs of their ancestors enacting the life of thousands of years ago. There is a back ground for you! How noble it made these fruit merchants for once; what distinction it gave them!" [9]

This theatre production performed by the Greeks at Hull House is credited as being the start of the little theatre concept in the United States.

A group of Greek wrestlers at Hull House Gymnasium, circa 1910.

"The club rents a large portion of the fourth floor in the Boys' Club Building, in addition to a room fitted up for athletics is a smaller one with Greek books and papers used as an office and lounge. They have maintained a fine standard in athletics. One of the members who has been most active in this club is now an instructor in wrestling and boxing at the University of Chicago." [10]

23

THE GREEKTOWN DELTA

"How many nights did I not stay awake while the interminable whine of Greek folk-music came across Halsted Street to my exasperated ears? Had not Miss Addams gathered Greeks by the hundred to come to the Theatre during their unemployment so that English words could be taught to them in chorus and en masse? The Greeks to her were a Presence, a possibility of no doubt of human suffering, but also a group that was suffused with reality for her, a group with a cluster of warm and ripened association. She felt the aura of Greece when she dealt with them. She had a heart for them, or rather an imagination for them, a grasp of their difficulties and their fractured loyalty." [11]

"There were eleven of us living under one roof. It was a three bedroom apartment with one bathroom."

Typical streetscapes in the Greektown neighborhood.

"It was just everybody got along. It's amazing. And I think basically it had to do with Hull House, because Hull House got these people together. Got the people to live together, got the people to get along together. It was just a nice neighborhood."

"Another inhabitant of the area, Al Capone, became almost as much of a local hero as Miss Addams. During the depression years, Al's henchmen used to hijack trucks off of the large grocery stores, park them in the Harrison-Halsted-Blue Island intersection, and pass out food to destitute immigrant families. Local police helped hungry men and women cart away their cases of corn and peas; they even directed traffic around the parked trucks."

"I remember on Thanksgiving Day–it must have been 1933 or 1934- when Al appeared in person to pass out turkeys "borrowed" from the "swells on Michigan Avenue." [12]

Typical street activity. "In 1894, there were but 77 Greeks in the Nineteenth Ward. In 1908, the number had increased to 576, and in 1914 there were resident in this ward 1,881 Greeks, the largest colony of that race in Chicago, and one of the largest in the United States."[23]

"In 1954...the stroller from Harrison and Halsted down Blue Island Avenue could not have failed to note the Kaffeneion houses, their elderly customers reading *Hellenikos Typos* over their Turkish coffee; for this was the 'Greek Delta.'" [13]

REMEMBERING GREEKTOWN

19th Ward - The largest settlement of Chicago Greeks is in the 19th ward, north and west of Hull House. Here is the Greek Orthodox Church, a school supervised by the priest in which thirty children are taught a little English, some Greek, much of the achievements of Hellas, and the obligation that rests on every Greek to rescue Macedonia from the Turks and the Bulgarians; here too, is the combination Greek bank, steamship-ticket office, notary public, and employment agency, and the coffee-houses, where the men drink black Greek coffee, play cards, speculate on the outcome of the next Greek lottery, and in the evening sing to the accompaniment of the Greek bag-pipes or as evidence of their Americanization—listen to the phonograph. On Halsted Street, south of Harrison, almost every store for two blocks has Greek characters on the windows, and recalling one's long-forgotten college Greek, one learns that the first coffee-house is the "Café Appolyon," and that their newspaper "The Hellas" is published next door. A block west on Blue Island Avenue one finds the "Parthenon Barber Shop" and the Greek drug store. If an American were to visit this neighborhood on the night of Good Friday when the stores are draped with purple and black and watch at midnight the solemn procession of Greek men marching down the street carrying their burning candles and chanting hymns, he would probably feel as though he were no longer in America, but after a moment's reflection he would say that this could be no place but America for the procession was headed by eight burly Irish-American policemen and along the walks were "Americans" of Polish, Italian, Russian Jewish, Lithuanian, and Puritan ancestry watching with mingled reverence and curiosity this celebration of Good Friday, while those who marched were homesick and mourning because "this was not like their Tripoli." [14]

Settling Greektown – No author has ever dated the exact moment when Chicago's Greektown came into being. Yet we do know that between 1880 and 1920, the massive waves of immigration that brought Greeks to North America arrived. We also know that the intersection of Halsted, Harrison, and Blue Island formed the absolute and indisputed heart of Chicago's Greektown. This intersection quickly became known as "The Delta district." As streams flow together to make a mighty river, the Greek Delta is said to have been created by the tumbling surge of Greeks into the district. Various authors and arguments outline a greater Greektown district, which eventually existed north to Randolph Street, south to Roosevelt Road, east toward the downtown Loop, and west all the way to Ashland Avenue. At its height, this greater Greektown district was reputedly the home of some 30,000 to 40,000 first- and second- generation Greeks. [14.5]

Greek Meeting – "On January 3rd Hull House in co-operation with the Greek Colony of Chicago, held a meeting which filled the Woman's Club Hall to its utmost capacity. In the last five years, since Greeks have been coming in large numbers to Chicago, they find that Americans make no distinction between them and other more ignorant immigrants from southern Europe. As the modern Greek is devoted to his own country and race, the Greek immigrant bitterly resents the criticism of his manners and habits in America by Americans who, he believes, disregard his historical background and traditions.

A committee of well-educated Greeks, therefore arranged with Miss Addams that an American-Greek meeting should be held in which Americans should speak in English of the glorious history of Greece, and the Greek speakers should tell their countrymen in their native tongue some of the duties and requirements of their adopted country.

This was to be an introductory meeting to pave the way for a series of exclusively Greek meetings in which freshly arrived immigrants were to be taught what was expected of them in this new country in return for the benefits and advantages which the country offers." [15]

THE IMMIGRANT EXPERIENCE

Dad - "My dad came over as a child of fourteen. Today you don't send a kid across the street to get a loaf of bread at fourteen. But, he was sent here by his parents because his father had three daughters, and in Greece, you must have a dowry to marry off your daughters. And, he had no money. They put him on a boat that went to Naples, Italy, and from Naples, it took him seventeen days to get to the United States. When he got to Ellis Island, he was going to some cousin's of his that lived in Richmond, Virginia. They had a shoe shining place. That was a big thing-shoe shining and hat cleaning for fedoras. So, he got aboard his train and the only thing he had was a blanket that his mother had woven for him. He hadn't had a bath in two weeks. And, you can imagine what he smelled like. He had this tag out telling, like a piece of mail, where he was going to. He had many different jobs all over the country. From shining shoes in Richmond, to selling flowers in Washington, D.C. to selling chestnuts on the streets of Harrisburg and up and down the coast. Eventually, he ended up in both Minneapolis, and Milwaukee, then Chicago working in the ice cream business."

–Ulysses Paul Backas

They Left Everyting - "They immigrated because the Turks were coming to their village in the Northern part of Thrace, which is Turkey now. And, they were coming there, and my grandfather was fighting against them in another part of Greece and he wrote to my grandmother and told her just to take the wagon and enough food for the trip, and to meet him at the seaside in Salonica at the pier. And, apparently that is what she did—left everything and took nothing. Just took enough clothes for the period and off they went."   *–Helen Georges*

It was was a very lonely life – "A life of an immigrant is very sad. Not being able to speak. Not being able to shop freely because you don't know how to ask for things. But, I was determined. I grew up in a bakery. My father had a bakery and it was hard work. If you were old enough to hold a broom, you swept the bakery. That's it, there's nothing else. So, it was difficult there. So, I was determined to make it, or else. And, that's how it was. A constant struggle to discipline yourself to learn the new ways of life. To meet wonderful Greek friends and other nationalities because I lived in a building that was the League of Nations. Any nationality that you could think of along, near Harrison, was there. And, you come from a country where everybody is the same in the village of 2,000 people. We know each other all of the time, and all of a sudden, there are different people. How can this be possible? And, they all live in harmony. That's the magic of America."

–Effie Gekas

The Boat Trip - "The boat from Athens was the 'Elosalem.' It took 14 days to get to New York. Katerina got very seasick and spent most of the time in her cabin. The ship was very dirty. She lost 15 pounds on the journey because all she could eat were apples and eggs. She remembers seeing frozen meat lying on the floor before they cooked it. She couldn't stomach the thought of eating it. She remembers taking her first shower on the boat. She told herself that life was going to be good in America. Upon entering New York harbor, the captain called everyone to deck. They all ran out and there was the Statue of Liberty. Everyone clapped, yelled and cried. 'We made it!' It was September 2, 1955."

–relative of Ekaterina Robakis Kouchoukos
of the village Lahanatha in Messinia, Greece

Making a Living - "My father came here before the turn of the century. He, like most immigrants, worked on the railroad and did a lot of menial jobs due to the lack of the ability to speak the language and any true formal education. He left the country at 13 and then he brought his younger brother when he got established there. And, from there they moved into pedaling vegetables and fruit. And, from there, he got into the candy business–ice cream parlor–and got involved in real estate at the same time. And, when he was 45, he retired, and that's when he went back to Greece and got married and started his family."

–George Dalianis

Continued from page 19
room and board. However, housing was usually located near crime-ridden neighborhoods and filled with prostitution and other vices. Because they were always working, these teenagers did not have time for school, evening classes or social organizations at venues like Hull House. But, this was a better life than being deported.

Greek men, married and unmarried, enjoyed coffee shops (or *kaffenia*) for socializing–unlike other immigrants, the Irish, Polish, or Italians, who congregated in saloons to socialize. These simple establishments, consisting of a few tables and chairs in a room in a wooden or two-story brick building, served as fraternal gathering places. Each of the more than 100 coffee shops in the Delta tended to represent a different region of Greece. These structures provided a social outlet for men to escape their crowded living conditions and interact with a family-like community network–a substitute for the rich experience of traditional family life in Greece.

Hellenic pride reverberated in these establishments. Men in dark mustaches spoke of news from their beloved Greece, expounded their philosophies to willing listeners, or kept current on events unraveling in their new home–Chicago and the United States. In these smoke-filled rooms, they played cards, drank coffee, and gregariously debated politics and business.

Also, several Greek newspapers organized, including the *Greek Star* in 1904 which celebrated 100 years of continuous publishing in 2004. The paper began in the Greek language, but slowly introduced English to help serve both as an educational tool to practice English, as well as to meet the needs of first- and second-generation immigrants.

While working in America, the men

At the Nick and Tom Maverick family store and shoe-shine parlor in 1914.

The Greek spirit of getting ahead was always present. "In those days, there were peddlers in the alleys of Chicago and they would holler out and women would come and they would buy food and vegetables."

"People didn't buy shoes every other week like they do now. They had a hat cleaner and a shoe shiner."

sent funds back home to provide family with better living conditions. Even though they did without, it was their duty to provide for families and unwed sisters. It was estimated that $5 million annually was sent back to Greece between 1903-1908, and between 1919-1928, over $52 million was transferred. This influx helped propel Greece's economic development, enabling the building of houses and churches, and providing valuable, yet intangible, import revenue.

At some point, a husband felt prosperous enough with an established business or secure employment to bring his family over to America. He either went back to Greece to make the return voyage with his family, or in most cases, purchased steamship tickets and welcomed them at the port.

With the arrival of more women, family life began to take root. Houses were tidy, children were clean and dressed neatly, and meals were pre-

pared. The cooking and cleaning no longer burdened the male provider. Economically, since fathers did not need to provide the traditional dowries for their unmarried daughters, their financial future brightened.

Unlike other ethnic groups in Chicago, Greek wives did not work in the factories or sweatshops that were being built in the newly, industrialized Chicago because Greek men thought it was a disgrace for women to work out-

Catching up on the day's events at Kynouria Coffee House.

"In Greektown, you would stop at the coffee houses. Going in, they talk to you. Tell you stories coming over from there to here, what they went through. A lot of them were bachelors."

Greektown grocers served not only the Greeks downtown, but also Greeks in the north or south sides of the city. Greektown was the place to purchase fresh staples like fruits and vegetables, lamb, and of course—bread.

side of the home. However, many wives did assist in their husband's place of business.

Women were also very instrumental in creating a framework for philanthropic work in both the United States and in Greece. Many helped in the war relief effort to send money, supplies, and clothing aid to Greece during their civil war in 1946. Also, women's groups such as GAPA (Greek American Philanthropic Association), with the support of meeting rooms supplied by Hull House, began their charitable work assisting other Greeks and Americans.

New Greek families coming over were now settling in areas of Chicago outside the downtown area. In 1904, on the South Side, another concentration of Greeks formed along 63rd Street between Wentworth and Cottage Grove in the Woodlawn district. Dotted with Greek shops and residences, the neighborhood soon organized a church and school, Sts. Constantine & Helen Greek Orthodox Church and Koraes School. And, in the early 1900s, the neighborhood around South

Central Avenue near what was then the last stop of the trolley from downtown Chicago was comprised of nearly all Greek immigrants who were shopkeepers and restaurateurs. In 1925, Assumption Church was founded to serve the city's Far-West Side.

Because three out of four men between the ages of 15 and 45 had emigrated from Greece, and later sent for their families, Greece lacked men. Therefore, when news of the Balkan War hit, the much-needed men went home to Greece in 1912 to help fight. In addition, Greeks living in America

"My mother never worked, she took care of us. That generation, it was a disgrace for the women to go to work. Now the Greeks that came after the war, the women went to work, they owned beautiful homes. They went back and forth to visit Greece. It made such a difference, after the war, when men weren't ashamed for their wives to work."

Preparing eggs in the home for the Greek Easter celebration.

"Because you come to a rich country, they think you are going to be wealthy. It isn't like that at all. You live in a small apartment, you economize to pay your rent, and to buy the necessities."

(some 60,000) fought for the United States in World War I. Through this service, they were able to obtain their U.S. citizenship.

By 1924, the immigration exodus had slowed due to the Immigration Quota Act and the Depression in the 1930s. During these devastating years, the majority of Greeks lost what equity they had built up in the United States, yet found it hard to return to their native homeland to pick up the pieces and begin again.

In 1946, a civil war broke out in Greece between the Communists and Greece's government forces. Many Greeks lost their homes and their villages were destroyed. Over one million refugees fled their towns and homeland.

In 1948, despite the quota restrictions, Congress passed a Displaced Person's Act which allowed Greeks to immigrate to the United States, thus giving some Greeks new opportunities to rebuild their lives in America.

But it was World War II and urban expansion beginning in the Greek Delta which caused the greatest change as Greek and other ethnic communities were no longer neighborhoods in isolation.

The period following the war was essentially a period of assimilation. Cultural, occupational, and territorial boundaries began to disappear.

Yet, throughout all the changes, the Greek community has retained many of the traditions which make it unique. It has grown a new image, but its foundation is its citizens, the sons and daughters of immigrants. People with a strong work ethic, a solid faith in God, and in each other. Proud of their heritage, they are still ready to show the world that they are Americans.

"Like all pioneers who come from the various countries of Europe to the United States the Greeks expect to return. Many of them are sending money home not only to support the wife and children they left behind them, but to buy land in Greece. But those who return, undoubtedly the great majority will find that ten or fifteen years in the United States has unfitted them for contented residence in Greece." [16]

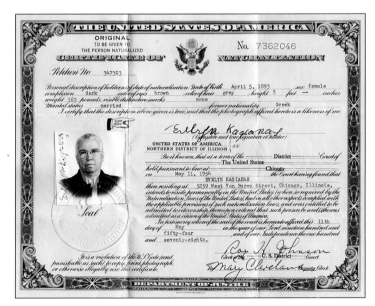

Becoming naturalized was an important passage for most Greek Americans. Evelyn Kagianes of 5259 West Van Buren became a U.S. citizen on May 11, 1954.

"There is nothing like this one [country] here. Where you have the freedom of expression, freedom of thought. If they ask me, 'Are you an American citizen?' I say, 'Yes, by choice.' I come to this country. I love this country. We are fortunate to be able to say that 'my heritage is Greek' and nobody's going to attack me for that."

George Phillos, at left, attends the Chicago World's Fair in 1933 with his nephew.

REMEMBERING EARLY TIMES

"Somewhere between the ages 12-14, in the early 1900's, a solicitor came to the village trying to get the young boys to come to the United States to layout railroad tracks. My father first worked as an errand boy. Then he got a job laying railroad tracks, followed by becoming a fruit peddler selling apples and oranges on street corners, and finally he opened up his own store. He had a very fine clientele, and with his own horse and wagon, he made the rounds of the alleys throughout the Chicago area delivering fruits and vegetables."

–*Jayne Terovolas*

Socrates schoolchildren gather for instruction. In the 1920s, it cost $5.00 per student to attend.

"They never went back. The town, the city they came from was taken over because of WWII. In those days, to take a trip to Greece took over ten days by ship. That's three weeks back and forth, and time off for the vacation. They couldn't afford it. So, they never went back."

–*James M. Mezilson*

"I came in a boat. It was very difficult to get the money for the ticket. And, if you had taken any money with you, you had to explain to the Greek authorities where you got the money. You had to complete a lot of forms. I came May 15th, 1949 and it took us 19 days. I came to New York. I borrowed $2.00 from a friend in the boat and I had with me two bottles of brandy. My intention was to call a friend of mine, however, a lady that was there said to me, 'Your aunt sent me to pick you up.' "

–*Michael Vlamis*

"My grandmother smiled at the Chicago Public School teacher, nodded toward her daughter [my mother], and said in her broken English, 'Her name Evangelia.' The child looked terrified, because the teacher scowled at her as she said, 'Her name is … what? Eva… lee…what? Who can spell that?' Grandmother smiled and calmly repeated her daughter's name as she tried to introduce her to her new teacher. The teacher looked at the child in exasperation and said, 'That name just won't do in an American classroom. We'll call you Lillian. Take a seat over there.' "

–*From the essay* Growing Up Greek in Chicago, 1919: A First Grader's Perspective *by Dr. Chakonas*

"In about 1912, my dad was about 19 years old, and he and two buddies were working together and they found out that Greece was fighting the Bulgarians and the Turks in the Balkan Wars of 1912-13. Now, here's three young men who left their country because the country couldn't support them, couldn't do anything for them. Greece couldn't give them an education, they hardly finished grammar school, but they felt patriotic enough to want to go back and fight. So, they each took two hundred dollars, which in those days was a lot of money, and they went to a man downtown that they trusted—he was a tailor. And, they each gave him two hundred dollars. They said, 'In case something happens to us in the war, send this two hundred dollars back to our mothers.' So, dad went over there and fought. He came back never to go back to Greece again."

–*Ulysses Paul Backas*

"She came from a family that was of medium means. She didn't have a dowry. There was no way a Greek was going to ask for her hand in marriage because she didn't have a dowry. So, that's why many of the females at that time came to this country and married. They did not have dowries, so they married Greek Americans who then brought them to this country."

–*Angela Gregory Paterakis*

Harry Lalagos in 1948 stands in front of the Pan Arcadian Federation headquarters in Greektown. Arcadia is a province in central Peloponnesus in southern Greece, and the city of Tripolis is its capital. The Arcadians who immigrated and stayed in America gathered with fellow Arcadians, forming syllogos (clubs) to exchange ideas about how they could help their villages in Greece. It is estimated that close to 30,000 Arcadians reside within the greater Chicago metropolitan area. In 1931, the Pan Arcadian Federation was formed to help coordinate all the village clubs comprised of Arcadians across the United States. There is a national convention each year and every four years the convention takes place in Tripolis, Arcadia. Philanthropic projects have included the building of the Pan Arcadian Hospital in 1950 in Tripolis as well as contributions to the Greek-American Nursing and Rehabilitation Center and the Hellenic Museum and Cultural Center.

"My greatest accomplishment was that I was able to bring my niece over and I helped bring quite a few people over from the old country and they are all good citizens."

–*Sophie R. Andrikopoulos*

Roasting lamb in the backyard of the Acropolis Restaurant and Tavern in the old Greektown neighborhood.

"We moved a fair amount those days back in the Depression. It was not uncommon to be moving around quite a bit. In many places they would offer one month's rent free when you moved in. So, I'm sure that at least on one occasion, we moved to take advantage of that situation. So, we were many years in one location, all on the south side, but we moved around so we probably weren't close to any individual except through the church."

–Constantine Katsaros

The West Randolph Street Market, otherwise known as Haymarket Square, photo opposite page, was a broad open space formed by the widening of West Randolph Street for an open-air produce market between Halsted and Des Plaines Street. It was a center of business activity for Greek peddlers, circa 1905. In 1886, this had been the site of the famous Haymarket Riot where Chicago unionists, reformers, socialists, anarchists, and ordinary workers joined in the national movement for a shorter, eight-hour work day.

Markets like the Randolph Street Market and the South Water Street Market served as hubs for the fruit and vegetable business, and Greeks in the business ultimately dominated the retail and wholesale business, competing mostly with the Italians. In 1904, there were confrontations with the Grocer's Association who fought the Greek peddlers because the grocers were forced to sell their food at higher prices due to paying store rents, and the grocers lost much business to the peddlers. In 1909 the Greeks surrounded City Hall with their fruit carts to protest an increase in the annual peddler's license from $25 to $200. Ultimately, this forced thousands of peddlers to open their own permanent stores and restaurants.

The Austin Lunch at 1458 West Madison Street in Chicago. Paul Limberopulos, proprietor, sits in the first counter chair—the other gentlemen are his employees.

"He worked long hours. You know, he was married had started to have a family, the depression hit, he lost his business, he lost everything. And then he went and worked for a company driving a laundry truck. He never went on public aid, there were just a lot of hardships."

–Helen Malevitis

"There was NO jobs whatsoever. Papa say he's hardly taking in ten dollars a day. Place was open 24 hours, he work more than sixteen... and only take in ten bucks. And from those ten bucks he's got to pay the rent, Charlie the cook, Al the waiter, Harry the dishwasher, Mrs. Feldman who sell the meat... the electricity, the gas, the water and more... I was positive we was gonna be [living] in the streets with ice and snow that winter."

–Excerpt is from Vasiliki Limberopulos from Austin Lunch, Greek-American Recollections, *speaking of her husband, Paul.*

There were several larger apartment buildings in the area and they housed many Greek families. This photo captures the children from one of the complexes near Halsted and Harrison streets. By having all of these families so close to one another, there were always enough children with which to play.

"I went to Bowen High School in South Chicago. Luckily, the government gave us three dollars a month for transportation. The streetcar would go on the side of the railroads and we would wait until one came. It was interesting. Streetcar people were nice too."

"Dad worked everyday from noon to midnight. But that wasn't the only thing, he would have to take the street car home from 92nd and Commercial. We lived at 63rd and Kedzie. Imagine the poor guy taking a street car having to change three times. A long journey home, you know."

"I remember the red brick Hull House well. My mother used to press three pennies in my hand and send my sister and me two blocks to the House, where we were showered, cleaned, and sent to an 'open air' room to dry off. Later, we spent our three pennies for a bowl of lentil soup, a bologna sandwich, and a glass of milk. I ate so many bologna sandwiches and so many bowls of lentil soup that I refuse to this day to have them in my house." [17]

Michael Spiro stands at the counter of his confectionery located at 5501 South Cottage Grove in Chicago in 1915.

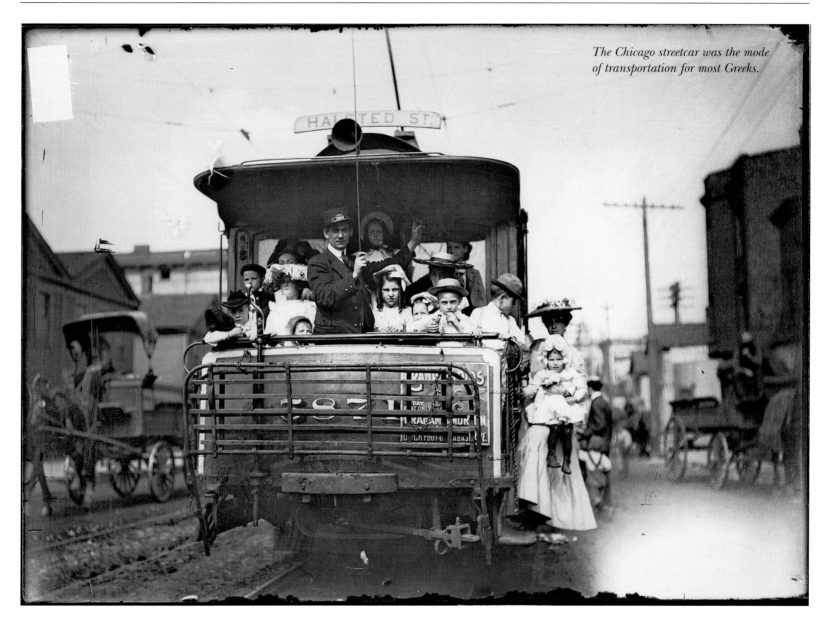

The Chicago streetcar was the mode of transportation for most Greeks.

" I used to take the street car from 63rd and Kedzie to 62nd and Michigan for Greek school with my sister. Class was from 4:00-6:00. And, then we took the street car home."

"In the early days, we didn't even have a phone in the house. Say, my mother wanted to visit so and so. We'd get on the streetcar and go there and if they were home, we got to visit them. And, if they weren't home, then we would leave and maybe go to someone else's house. That's the way they did it then."

Outside the Blue Goose Market in 1932. Located at 3816 North Broadway, shop proprietor John T. Sfondouris holds his daughter, Georgia Sfondouris Mitchell, and stands next to his wife, Merope, and son, Nick.

"We had to go to school, work in the grocery store, and go to Greek School, so we didn't have any time to get into mischief."

"I worked all my life, seven days a week–12, 13, 14 hours a day. I could not do everything I wanted to do. I sacrificed. When my friends were going out and doing things and taking vacations, I wasn't. And, one of my regrets is that I didn't take enough time off from my business. I thought the business couldn't get along without me."

"The best part of owning your own business? Well, like anything else, the challenges. I mean, there are long days, and there's times when it can be a little bit stressful, but I guess the bottom line is being able to determine your own destiny. You can make your own decisions, and hopefully see the fruits of your labor."

Inside the Blue Goose Market, Nick J. Sfondouris rides his tricycle while parents John T. and Merope Sfondouris interact with the butcher and a customer.

The demolition of Hull House in 1963 along with much of the Greektown Delta neighborhood. The city was embarking on a major redevelopment phase to make room for the University of Illinois and several major expressways. It was the end of an era: the knock on the door, the offer of a "fair market value." Such was the fate of all Greektown residents. The neighborhood was leveled. The dislocated residents missed "the friends who used to gather in front of their homes" to chat away the afternoon, or cool off in the evenings. The children missed their playmates.

Life was quiet on their new street. No Greek music, no smells of Greek cooking emanating from the kitchens, no recanting stories of the motherland. No epitaphio proceeding past their home on Good Friday. Life would never be the same.

FAMILY RECIPES

For the Greeks, religion and customs are synonymous, and embody a way of life. Family pride and tradition are priorities in the Greek household. Food is a major component of these elements, and not just as sustenance, but also as a means of bringing people together. There is no greater joy for a Greek than to host someone at their table. Pairing good food and wine, with good company is considered one of the great joys of life.

Each Greek region, and consequently Chicago immigrants from those areas, have individualized traditional dishes, adding their own special accents. From one house to the next, even a simple chicken dinner can be an entirely new and exciting experience.

In the following pages, members of Chicago's Greek community share their favorite recipes, some passed down from generations, so you may bring the warmth and enjoyment of Greek cooking into your home.

Kali Orexi ! (Bon Appetit)

DOLMADES
(STUFFED GRAPE LEAVES)

A family favorite, and one that, for many, epitomizes Greek life and Greek cuisine.

INGREDIENTS

1 large jar Orlando California grape leaves (ethnic food stores)
3 pounds lean ground lamb or beef (I grind my own)
2 eggs
1/4 cup rice
1 large onion (minced and sauté in 6 tbsp. olive oil in
*   separate pan, cool, then add onions and oil to mixture)*
4 tbsp. olive oil
1 small bunch fresh parsley chopped or 2 tsp. dry
1 small bunch fresh anise chopped or 2 tsp. dry
6 - 8 leaves fresh basil chopped or 1 tsp. dry
6 - 8 leaves fresh mint chopped or 1 tsp. dry
1 tsp. salt
1/4 tsp. black pepper
1/4 tsp. nutmeg

EGG LEMON SAUCE:

5 eggs
3 lemons (always use fresh
*   lemon juice)*
1 1/2 cups broth from dolmades
1/2 tsp. salt
A pinch of white pepper

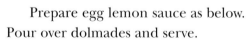

In a large pot, pour 4 tablespoons olive oil. Heat well, then place aside. In a large bowl, add the ground meat, and the rest of the ingredients. Mix well by hand. Rinse leaves thoroughly and drain in a colander. Take one leaf at a time, and place it on a plate, shiny side down. Put one tablespoon of the meat mixture on the leaf. Bring sides of the leaf over, then roll to create each dolma. Arrange dolmades in the pot over the heated oil, in a circle formation. When finished, add enough water to cover the dol-

mades (about 2 cups). Cover the pot with a dish large enough to cover the surface of the dolmades (to keep them from unfolding, as they cook in the pot). Cook at medium-to-low heat for 1 hour and 15 minutes. If you are using a pressure cooker, cook for 20 minutes. When done, drain the broth from the pot by tilting it and holding the dolmades in the pot with the plate. Reserve the broth. Place the dolmades in a serving dish. Keep them hot until 15 minutes before serving.

Prepare egg lemon sauce as below. Pour over dolmades and serve.

Serves 8-10 as a main course, 20-25 as a side dish.

EGG LEMON SAUCE

Heat the broth from the dolmades in a small pot, then simmer on low heat. Beat 5 eggs in a blender for 1 minute. Add juice from 3 lemons, 1/2 tsp. salt and a pinch of white pepper. Slowly pour the egg lemon mixture into the broth, stirring constantly until it begins to thicken.

CATHY GOFIS

SPICY BAKED SHRIMP AND MACARONADA

INGREDIENTS

2 pounds jumbo shrimp, tail on,
  cleaned, and butterflied
1 1/2 cups olive oil, extra virgin
  (Kalamata preferred)
3 cups tomato sauce
28 oz. can peeled whole tomatoes,
  rough chopped, drained
6 cloves garlic, sliced
1 cup chicken broth
Zest of 1 lemon
Juice of 1 lemon
1 tbsp. red wine vinegar
1 tbsp. sugar
1 tbsp. oregano – Greek
1 tsp. crushed red pepper flakes
1/4 lb. crumbled Feta cheese
Sea salt to taste
Black pepper to taste
Parsley to garnish (optional)
1-500 g. package spaghetti,
  Greek macaronada or
  your favorite pasta
1 tsp. cinnamon
1 tsp. nutmeg
1/4 cup grated Kefalotiri cheese
  (or subsitute Parmesan)

This dish comes from the small town of Kynegou, where my father's family lives. My family uses this dish for anything from lunch to holidays. The simplicity yet extraordinary richness of shepherds and farmers that live there is reflected in this dish. It only requires two pots and an oven, but is filled with layers of spice and flavor. When making this dish I will sometimes substitute different cheeses or pastas. But, I never sacrifice on the quality of olive oil or the amount.

Preheat oven to 375 degrees. In a large pan or skillet, combine 1 cup oil, tomato sauce, tomatoes, garlic, broth, oregano, vinegar, lemon juice, lemon zest, crushed pepper, and sugar. Stir and place in oven, uncovered, for 1 hour. Stir after 1/2 hour and adjust seasoning using sea salt and black pepper to taste.

Meanwhile, cook pasta in boiling salt water until al dente. Drain. Put pasta back into pot and toss with 1/2 cup oil, nutmeg, cinnamon and grated cheese. Place in oven and bake until slightly brown, approximately 10 minutes.

Remove sauce from oven. Place shrimp on top with crumbled Feta. Return to oven and cook until shrimp are tender and cheese is slightly brown, approximately 10-15 minutes, depending on the size of the shrimp.

Transfer pasta to a serving bowl and ladle sauce over it. Put shrimp on top. Garnish with grated cheese, lemon wedges, and parsley.
Serves 4-6.

PAUL BOUNDAS

EGG LEMON SOUP

Combine chicken, salt, pepper, and 3 quarts of water into large pot. Bring chicken to a boil covered, then cover askew to reduce the broth a bit. Boil until the meat starts to fall off the bone, approximately one hour. Skim the froth off of the boiling water and dispose. Let the meat cool. Skin and debone the chicken.

Put the College Inn chicken broth into the pot with the existing broth and bring it to a boil. Add rice and boil covered for 20 minutes (longer for softer rice.) Crack the eggs into a separate bowl. Squeeze the lemon juice from 3 lemons and combine with 3 whole eggs and blend. Cut up chicken thoroughly.

While constantly stirring the eggs and lemon, add the broth slowly–a ladle at a time, while at the same time kissing the air. This seemingly benign action of kissing the air will keep the mixture from curdling, according to grandmother.

Pour the egg-lemon-broth mixture back into the pot with the rice and add the chicken. Salt and pepper to taste and add some more lemon if desired. Serves 6-8. Enjoy!

THE VERY REVEREND ARCHIMANDRITE DEMETRI KANTZAVELOS

INGREDIENTS

1/2 chicken with skin

3 large organic lemons–room temperature (roll firmly on the counter to break up the lemon fiber and provide more juice)

3 large eggs–room temperature

48 oz. College Inn Chicken Broth

1 1/2 cups Uncle Ben's converted rice (add more if you desire thicker soup, add less if you desire thinner soup)

1 tsp. pepper

1 tsp. salt

KOURAMBIEDES

As college friends, we were always welcome at the home of my close friend and koumbara, Alice Kopan. Her mother, Tula Orphanas, always treated us to her delectable kourambiedes. This is her recipe, which I have used ever since. A popular, melt-in-your-mouth dish that graces the Greek sweets table at every holiday or festive occasion.

INGREDIENTS

1 lb. unsalted butter
1/2 cup powdered sugar
2 egg yolks
1 oz. anisette (or brandy, or ouzo)
5 cups cake flour, sifted
1 cup almonds or nutmeats (optional)

To begin, cream butter until very light. Gradually beat in sugar. Add egg yolks and anisette. Mix well, then gently fold in flour to create dough. Shape into 1-inch round balls. Place on ungreased cookie sheet and bake in a preheated oven at 350 degrees for 20 minutes. Transfer cookies to wax paper lightly coated with powdered sugar. Sprinkle liberally with more powdered sugar.

Yields 6 dozen cookies.

MAE PANOPLOS

FASOLAKIA
(VEGETABLE DISH)

This recipe comes from my mother who was from the village of Doxa Gortinias in Arcadia, Greece. It is a dish which is easy to make, especially in the summer when vegetables are plentiful. Traditionally eaten as the main course, it was served with freshly baked bread and Feta cheese. Today, this recipe can be served next to a main meat dish such as lamb, pork, beef, chicken, or even fish.

INGREDIENTS

3 lbs. fresh cut string beans

2 lbs. small whole round potatoes, peeled

1 medium-sized onion, diced

1 cup olive oil

1 – 14.5 oz. can diced tomatoes

1/2 cup water

1 – 15 oz. can tomato sauce

1/2 cup chopped parsley

1 medium-sized zucchini, diced

salt and pepper to taste

Sauté onions in oil for 5 minutes. Add string beans and sauté for an additional 5 minutes. Add diced tomatoes and tomato sauce. Bring to a boil. Add potatoes, zucchini, water, salt, and pepper. Stirring occasionally, continue boiling over medium heat until vegetables are cooked. Sprinkle with chopped parsley and serve hot.

Serves 4 as a main course; 10 as a side dish.

VICKI FOUNTAS

MELOMAKARONA

Melomakarona are also known as Greek Honey Cookies. The name of "honey cookies" comes from dipping the cookies into a warm honey syrup after baking.

Preheat oven to 350 degrees. Sift the flour and baking powder together. Set aside. In another bowl, with a mixer on medium speed, cream the oil, Crisco, and sugar. In a measuring cup, pour in orange juice, then add baking soda and dissolve. Add to the oil mixture. Add brandy. Continue to mix. Remove from the mixer. Fold in rind, spices, chopped nuts, then flour. For a soft dough, knead slightly to blend all ingredients.

Shape small oval cookies, then flatten slightly with a fork. Place on ungreased cookie pans. Bake 20 to 30 minutes, then allow to cool.

Meanwhile, in a saucepan, combine water, honey, and sugar. Bring to a boil, then let boil for 5 minutes. Skim the foam from the top. Dip cookies in the warm syrup, 5-6 at a time. Remove the cookies with a slotted spoon.

Sprinkle with ground walnuts and cinnamon and transfer to a platter. Cookies can be stored in a tin for up to one month without requiring refrigeration. Yields 5 dozen cookies.

MARY KAMBANIS

INGREDIENTS
1-1/2 tbsp. Crisco
2 cups corn oil (Mazola)
Grated rind from one orange
1/2 cup orange juice
1/2 tsp. baking soda
7-1/2 to 8 cups cake flour
1 cup sugar
1/4 cup brandy
1/2 cup chopped walnuts
1 tsp. ground cinnamon
1/2 tsp. ground cloves
1/2 tsp. fresh ground nutmeg
1 1/2 tsp. baking powder

SYRUP TO GARNISH:
2 cups honey
Ground walnuts
2 cups sugar
Cinnamon
2 cups water

PAXIMATHIA
(TEA BISCUITS)

After a funeral in Greece, it is customary to serve brandy, coffee, and paximathia. Since rich desserts are not appropriate to this occasion, this is a cookie that is dry in texture and not too sweet. In America, it is served as part of the funeral meal (makaria). Now it is a popular treat throughout the year since it freezes well. Think of it as Greek biscotti.

INGREDIENTS

1 lb. butter

4 eggs

1 1/2 cups sugar

1 1/2 tsp. baking powder

1 1/2 tsp. baking soda

6-7 cups flour (measure before sifting)

1 tsp. vanilla

1/4 tsp. salt

2 tsp. anise seed, crushed

1 egg, beaten

sesame seeds

Cream butter and sugar, well. Add four eggs, one at a time, beating well with each addition. Add vanilla, then stir in flour, baking powder, baking soda, salt, and anise seed. Shape into 8 or 9 loaves and place on greased cookie sheets. Loaves should measure 3-4 inches wide, and with a height of approximately 1/2 inch. Beat the final egg, and then brush on each loaf. Sprinkle with sesame seeds, then bake for 15 minutes, in a 350-degree oven.

Remove from the oven, and immediately slice into 1/2-inch thick slices. When cooled, place paximathia on their sides on cookie sheets. Return to the oven for about 10 to 15 minutes, until slightly browned.

Yields approximately 150 cookies.

MARY T. KOULOGEORGE

GALAKTOBOURIKO
(GREEK CUSTARD PASTRY)

Galaktobouriko has been my favorite Greek pastry ever since I was a little girl. My mother never made it so, when I began to bake, I tried several recipes until I developed one I thought tasted the best. The funny thing is, this is now my husband's favorite, so in our household, this treat does not last long!

INGREDIENTS

6 eggs
1 1/2 cups sugar
1 1/2 tbsp. vanilla
1 cup Farina
8 cups milk
1 lb. commercial phyllo
    pastry sheets*
1/2 lb. sweet, unsalted
    butter, melted

SYRUP:

1 1/2 cups sugar
2 cups water
1/2 tsp. vanilla

*Follow package directions for thawing. Unwrap and lay pastry flat on table. Place one sheet of plastic wrap on the phyllo and a damp towel on top of the plastic. Each time you remove a sheet, cover phyllo with plastic wrap and the damp towel to keep it from drying out.

In a large bowl, use an electric mixer to combine eggs and sugar for about 3 minutes, or until creamy. Add vanilla and blend. Using a wooden spoon, gradually stir as you add Farina, and mix well.

Boil milk in a 4-quart saucepan, over medium heat. While stirring the egg mixture, slowly add hot milk. Pour the entire mixture into a large pot and cook on low heat, stirring often until the mixture thickens (it should look like creamy mashed potatoes). Remove from heat and continue stirring. Allow to cool.

Place 8 phyllo sheets, one at a time, in a buttered 9x12-inch baking pan. Brush each sheet with melted butter, to keep it from drying out. Allow sheets to cover bottom and sides of the pan. Pour in the custard mixture. Fold in any phyllo hanging over the edges of the pan. One at a time, place 8 more phyllo sheets on top of the custard, brushing each sheet with melted butter. With a sharp knife, cut top layers of phyllo into diamond shapes. Bake at 375 degrees for one hour, until golden brown.

To prepare syrup, boil water, sugar and vanilla over a low flame for 15 minutes. Pour warm syrup slowly over the cooked galaktobouriko, or cold syrup on warm pastry will work too.

Yields 20-24 pieces.

EVELYN KAKALETRIS-SCHAP

IMAM BAILDI

Both of my parents, though Greek, were born in Turkey, so growing up the cuisine in our home always had a Turkish influence. Imam Baildi, which in Turkish means "the Iman fainted" (because as my mother explained, the food was so very delicious). This has always been a family favorite.

Peel alternating strips of eggplant, and then slice crosswise, into 1/2-inch slices. Place into a container filled with water and about 1 tablespoon salt. Allow that to sit for 1 hour. Slice onion in half from top to root end, then in thin lengthwise slices. Coarsely chop garlic. In a large pot, sauté onions and garlic in 2 tablespoons olive oil, until wilted. Remove from the pan and set aside. Rinse and drain eggplant slices. Place 2 tablespoons oil in the bottom of the pot, then add about 1/3 of the eggplant slices. On top of this, place 1/3 of the onion/garlic mixture, 1/3 of the parsley, 2 tablespoons oil, salt, and pepper. Continue layering until all ingredients are used. Dilute tomato paste with water, and then add to mixture. Simmer for 45 minutes to one hour on a low heat. Add more water if needed. Serve at room temperature with some fresh, crusty Greek bread.

Serves 4-6 as a main course or 8-10 as a side dish.

ROSE DALIANIS

INGREDIENTS
2 medium eggplants
2 large onions
6 cloves garlic
1/2 cup olive oil
1/2 cup chopped parsley
1 6 oz. can tomato paste
2 cups water
salt and pepper

PASTITSIO

Bechamel sauce: Make this first so it has ample time to cool. In a 2-quart saucepan, bring milk to a boil. In a separate 2-quart saucepan, melt butter and slowly stir in cake flour, until it forms a smooth paste. Add hot milk. Stir continuously over a low flame until it thickens. Set aside to cool.

Pasta: Boil macaroni in salted water. (Do not overcook.) Drain and let stand while you prepare the meat sauce.

Meat sauce: In a large skillet, cook onions in 1/8 cup water until transparent. Add ground meat and 2 sticks cinnamon. Cook until meat is lightly browned. Add diluted tomato paste, and stir well. Add cinnamon, nutmeg (you should be able to taste a nice amount of these), then salt and pepper to taste. Cook slowly until the meat is cooked and most of the water has been absorbed. Remove from heat.

Combine: Place macaroni back into large pot, then add meat mixture. Blend well. In a separate bowl, beat 10 egg whites with 3 egg yolks, and add to this mixture. Slowly mix well (use your hands for best results). Add 1 cup grated cheese, and continue to mix.

Bake: Spread the meat/macaroni mixture into an 11-1/2-inch x 16-1/2-inch baking pan. Sprinkle 1 cup of grated cheese and some cinnamon over the top. Beat the remaining 7 egg yolks in a large bowl. Slowly add the cooled Bechamel sauce to the beaten yolks. If it's too thick, add a little milk while beating. Spread evenly over the meat/macaroni mixture. Bake at 375 degrees for 1 hour. Test center with a knife. Let stand 1 hour before cutting. Serves 16.

For a smaller serving, this recipe is easily cut in half. Also, you can prepare this ahead of time, freeze, then thaw and bake when you are ready to serve.

ELAINE KATZIORIS, MOTHER ANTONEA MALLERIS, AND DAUGHTER NICOLE LOUISE

INGREDIENTS

4 lbs. ground beef
1/8 cup water
3 large onions chopped fine
2 lbs. macaroni
2 sticks cinnamon
1 can tomato paste, mixed
  with 2 cups water
2 cups grated Myzithra cheese
2-1/2 sticks butter
10 eggs, separated
2 qts. milk
1-1/2 cups cake flour
Cinnamon and nutmeg
Salt and pepper to taste

YIAYIA MARY LALAGOS' FAMOUS KOULOURIA

INGREDIENTS

1 lb. butter and 1/4 stick margarine

4 cups sugar

14 eggs

1/2 cup milk (2 % is o.k.)

Scraped peel of 2 oranges and 1 lemon

6 tsp. liquid imitation vanilla

2 tbsp. baking powder

1/2 cup orange juice (no pulp)

1 1/2 tsp. baking soda

4 shots whiskey

*1 bag Ceresota unbleached flour,
     plus extra*

1/4 cup corn oil (Mazola or Wesson)

With a mix master on medium speed, and in a very large bowl, cream butter and margarine. Add sugar and mix together for about 5 minutes. Add 12 eggs. Once mixed in, add the milk. Scrape the peel of the oranges and lemon. Add to the mixture. Pour in vanilla, and add baking powder. Continue to mix. In a separate bowl or glass, pour orange juice. Drop in baking soda, and let foam for about one minute. Pour it into the mixture. Add whiskey. Keep mixing.

Begin adding flour, one cup at a time. After the 4th or 5th cup, you won't be able to use the mixer anymore, as you will have too much dough. Start kneading the dough, turning the sides in, turning it upside down. Add additional flour as needed, until dough is not sticky. After the 6th or 7th cup of flour, you should almost be there! The amount of flour can vary, based on how liquid-y the butter was at the beginning, or if you used additional vanilla, or more or less whiskey. Because of this, you will sometimes use an entire bag, sometimes less, sometimes more. Use your judgment. Dough should not stick to your fingers. When finished, move the dough to the center of the bowl. Lightly pour the oil around the dough, and work it into the dough. This is what makes the cookies malako, or soft.

Cover the dough with a towel and let it rest for about 10 minutes. Preheat the oven to 325 degrees. Grease cookie sheets. Roll the dough into thin "tubes." Twirl them into twist shapes, curl them into "S" shapes or "O" shapes. In a small bowl, beat two eggs. Using a pastry brush, brush each cookie with egg before placing in the oven. Bake for 8-10 minutes, until golden brown on the bottom. Transfer to a cooling rack. By all means, sample one, but they'll taste even better the next day, when the flavor has a chance to really set in!

Yields about 250 cookies.

MARIA FOTINOPOULOS

XEROTIGANA

My parents both came from the island of Crete. This is my mother's recipe. She made these for every festive occasion. When we lost her, my father started to make them. They are a favorite of the entire family which has extended to our grandchildren also.

Beat eggs with whisk. Add other liquid ingredients and salt. Slowly add flour, beating until it requires hands to mix. Keep adding flour and mix with hands until dough is soft and not too sticky. Knead dough on counter for about 5 to 7 minutes. Let dough rest, covered for 1/2 hour. Divide into 6 balls. Flour surface and dough. With rolling pin, roll out one ball at a time into a thin circle. Using an edged pastry cutter, cut into one-inch strips. Take strip and wrap loosely around hand a few times, stretching the dough a little. Secure with 2 toothpicks. Carefully drop into 350-degree corn oil, using 2 forks to keep dough circular. Do not fry more than 2 at a time. Turn xerotigana over in oil a few times. Fry until they turn a light brown. Drain on paper towel, remove toothpicks, dip into cooled syrup for a minute and sprinkle with chopped nuts. Finish all the strips and begin with next dough ball. Makes about 60.

Syrup: Bring sugar, water, cloves, and cinnamon to a boil. Boil for 20 minutes; add the lemon juice, boil a few more minutes. Allow to cool.

OLGA PAXINOS

INGREDIENTS

3 large eggs
8 oz. freshly squeezed orange juice
3 oz. corn oil
Pinch of salt
2 oz. ouzo or Masticha liqueur
Enough all purpose flour to make a soft dough (3-4 cups)
Corn oil for deep frying
2 cups chopped walnuts

SYRUP:

5 cups sugar
3 cups water
1 stick cinnamon
6 cloves
Juice of one lemon

CHICKEN KAPAMA

Growing up Greek Orthodox, we celebrate the coming of Lent (Apokrias) on Meatfare Sunday (eight Sundays before Easter) with this special dish. According to the teachings of our faith, Meatfare Sunday is the last Sunday prior to Easter that the Greek Orthodox congregation can eat meat. This is a tradition that we have continued to practice with our grandchildren. We serve this dish, which is very popular in our family, many times during the year.

INGREDIENTS

4 tsp. olive oil
1 onion, finely chopped
3 tsp. fresh garlic, finely chopped
1 tsp. tomato paste
1 whole chicken, cut in small pieces
1/2 tsp. pepper
1 tsp. salt

1/2 tsp. oregano
1 cinnamon stick
1 - 28 oz. can whole tomatoes, crushed by hand or 1 lb. fresh tomatoes, chopped
28 oz. water

Heat oil in a large sauté pan. Add garlic and onion, then cook for 15-30 seconds. Add tomato paste and chicken. Braise chicken, on both sides, until slightly colored. Add salt, pepper, oregano, cinnamon stick, tomatoes, and water. Cover and let cook for about 1 to 1-1/2 hours over medium heat, stirring occasionally. Remove chicken and place on a serving platter. Serve sauce (pan juices) on the side. Serve with macaroni and sprinkled Myzithra cheese. Serves 6.

BILL AND MARY KAKAVAS

MACARONADA
(GREEK SPAGHETTI WITH BURNT BUTTER)

Due to our busy schedules today, I decided to share a very simple recipe handed down from my mother. This recipe can be a hit in your household as it has been in mine for over 38 years. I sometimes serve the spaghetti (or pasta of your choice) without the meat as a side dish with roast or grilled lamb, pork, or beef. I also create it as a meat dish by adding ground meat. I always get raves no matter how I serve it.

INGREDIENTS

2 lbs. of your favorite pasta
2 sticks butter (no substitutes)
1/2 to 1 cup grated sharp Romano
    or Myzithra cheese
1/4 tsp. salt

OPTIONAL MEAT SAUCE:

2 lbs. lean ground meat
4 tbsp. oil
1 large onion, chopped
1/4 tsp. ground cinnamon
1 tsp. sugar
2 - 4 oz. cans tomato sauce
salt and pepper to taste

Hint: The secret is the caramelizing, or burning, of the butter. Too often, the butter is cooked or melted only to a golden yellow when in fact it must be brown. However, you must also be careful not to overcook or blacken (carbonize) the butter.

In a large pot, bring water and salt to a boil. Add pasta, stirring occasionally, so that it doesn't stick together. Cook for approximately 12 minutes. Drain when cooked. Do not rinse.

In a separate pot, over a medium heat, begin melting butter. The butter will start to boil just about the time the pasta is ready. The butter will go through a process as it boils. As it begins to melt, it will turn a golden yellow. As it begins to boil, it will get darker. It will them foam and start to rise. At this point, stir, and continue to do so, until the foam disappears. Keep stirring, until the butter turns brown, in the final stage. You will know that the butter is ready when you pour some on a piece of pasta, and it sizzles, then burns to a crisp.

You must work quickly now. Put half the drained pasta into a serving dish. Sprinkle with the grated cheese. Add the remaining pasta, and sprinkle this with cheese. Spoon the brown butter evenly over the top of the mixture. You should now have brown sprinkles everywhere, from the butter and cheese combination. Serve immediately.

Meat sauce: You may add this sauce if you wish. Remember, this is a dry sauce, unlike other pasta sauces, which are liquid.

Heat oil in a skillet. Sauté onions until transparent. Add ground meat and stir until the meat is brown. Add all the dry spices and tomato sauce and mix. Cook about 45 minutes to 1 hour, stirring occasionally, until the liquid is completely absorbed. Serves 6-8.

MARY CHRISTOFIDIS

TIROKAFTERI
(SPICY CHEESE SPREAD)

I remember the dishes my family used to prepare in Greece and the delicious appetizers that we would arrange when entertaining friends and relatives. One of them was tirokafteri but we had never attempted to make it ourselves. However, when my cousins would return from Macedonia in northern Greece, they always brought some back with them. I loved the taste, but I was utterly disappointed when I realized that this appetizer was not at all common in Athens. Years later, I heard a friend describe the tirokafteri recipe to a Chicago chef. I took a mental note of the recipe and after altering (mostly adding) a couple of new ingredients, I made this version for the first time. Since then, friends in Chicago and Athens have always complimented me for my tirokafteri. Because of this, I decided to share it with you. I am in the picture with my daughters, Sophie (orange shirt) and Emilia (green shirt).

INGREDIENTS

1 lb. Feta cheese
1 tbsp. strained yogurt
White pepper to taste
Pinch of salt
Pinch of sugar
More than a pinch of oregano
1 to 2 slices sun-dried tomatoes
1 banana pepper
3 to 4 oz. extra virgin olive oil

Using a fork, mash the Feta together with the oil, salt, pepper, sugar and oregano. Submerge sun-dried tomatoes in warm water for 15 minutes, to hydrate. Mince tomato and banana pepper, then add them to cheese mixture. Fold in strained yogurt to add creaminess and take away some of the heat from the pepper.

Hint: I like to prepare this one day prior to serving, then store it in the refrigerator until ready to serve. This gives the flavors the opportunity to blend together. Remove from the refrigerator about 30 minutes before serving. Serve with some crusty Greek bread or as a cheese supplement to a Greek village (horiatiki) salad.

Serves 4-6 in appetizer portions.

THEO RIGOPOULOS

56

GREEK ORZO SALAD

This recipe for Orzo-Feta salad signals the arrival of summer at my home, and the upcoming festivities of outdoor concerts on the lawn at Ravinia and Millennium Park. Although the recipe for this dish was not handed down from my Yiayia, the ingredients symbolize my Greek heritage. This dish is always requested by family and friends when preparing for our summer outings.

INGREDIENTS

SALAD:

1 lb. Orzo pasta
6 plum tomatoes, chopped
1/2 cup red onion, chopped
1/2 lb. Kalamata olives, sliced
1 lb. Feta cheese, crumbled
1 large or 2 small zucchinis, chopped

DRESSING:

1 medium garlic clove, minced
1 cup red wine vinegar
1/4 cup of olive oil
1 tsp. dried basil
1 tsp. oregano

Cook pasta according to directions on package, omitting any oil and salt. Drain and rinse. Combine pasta with tomatoes, onion, olives, Feta, and zucchini in a large bowl. Toss well.

Whisk together garlic, vinegar, olive oil, basil, and oregano in a small bowl. Pour dressing over pasta mixture, and toss well. Cover and chill if desired. Serves 4 as a main dish and 8 as a side dish.

SANDRA GANAKOS

FASOLOSALATA
(WHITE BEAN SALAD)

During my last visit to Greece, a family I visited served this salad. I liked it so much, I asked the hostess for the recipe. She provided me with a list of ingredients, but she was vague on the exact proportions of each ingredient. When I returned to Chicago, I reconstructed the salad from memory and it came out just as I remembered it.

INGREDIENTS
SALAD:

1 can (15 oz.) cannellini or
    great northern beans
1/4 cup red onion, thinly sliced
1/4 cup green pepper, diced

DRESSING:

2-3 tbsp. extra virgin olive oil
1-2 tbsp. lemon juice
salt and pepper to taste

Drain and rinse beans in cold water. Combine all ingredients. Mix well and adjust dressing to taste. Let stand 1-2 hours to allow flavors to blend. Garnish with whole Kalamata olives and quartered hard-boiled eggs. Serve with crusty bread. Serves approximately 3 luncheon-sized servings.

MATA COLOVOS-HANSEN

SAUSAGE OF NEW ANGHIALOS

This is one of my favorite recipes, and one that allows me to cook outside on the grill!

Mix all the ingredients for the marinade and whisk. Cut the sausages horizontally on one side, then open the sausages and lay them flat. Dip them in the marinade, and transfer to a plate. Cover and refrigerate overnight.

Preheat grill to 400 degrees. Grill both sides of the sausage until brown (approximately 20 minutes). Slice sausages into small pieces and place in a large mixing bowl. Add garnish ingredients and toss. Serve with toasted pita bread and sliced tomatoes.

Serves 6.

DINO DIMOPOULOS

INGREDIENTS

2 lbs. Greek sausage (bratwurst or Italian sausage)

MARINADE:

1/2 cup extra virgin olive oil
1/2 cup white wine
2 tbsp. Worcestershire sauce
1 tbsp. garlic powder
1 tbsp. onion powder
1/2 tsp. salt
1 tsp. paprika
1 tbsp. oregano
1/4 cup lemon juice

GARNISH:

1 red onion, thinly sliced
Chopped cilantro to taste
1/4 cup balsamic vinegar
1/2 cup extra virgin olive oil

STIFADO
(BEEF STEW WITH ONIONS)

My mother brought this recipe with her from her village of Meligala, Messinia in the early 1900s. This recipe is a rich, hearty dish, usually prepared with rabbit or pheasant during the fall and winter as I recall in my childhood home of Bayard, Nebraska. We like to serve it with a large bowl of creamy mashed potatoes, tossed Greek salad, Feta cheese, Kalamata olives, huge slices of crusty Greek bread, and wine. The aroma of this dish is all you need to bring the family to the table.

INGREDIENTS

5 to 6 lbs. stewing beef cut into
    2 or 3-inch slices

7 to 8 lbs. small (golf ball-sized) onions,
    cleaned and scored

1/2 cup extra virgin olive oil

1 – 4 oz. can plus 1 tbsp. tomato paste

1/2 cup red wine vinegar (or cider vinegar)

1/2 cup red wine

5 to 6 garlic cloves

1 tsp. whole pickling spices

1 large bay leaf

1 cinnamon stick

1/2 tsp. dried rosemary

1 tsp. sugar

Salt and pepper to taste

1 cup water

To begin, sauté beef in oil until browned. Season with salt and pepper, then remove beef from saucepan, and set aside. Combine sugar with the drippings to caramelize the mixture. Add onions and sauté until golden. Remove onions and return beef to pan. Place onions on top of beef.

Next, mix the tomato paste, wine, wine vinegar, and water, then add to saucepan. Place the garlic, spices, and herbs in a spice bag and place with beef and onions. Cover and simmer for two to three hours on top of stove or bake in a 275 degree oven, adding more water if necessary. Immediately remove spice bag when done. Serves eight. Hint: If fresh onions are not available, frozen onions can be used, but do not score them.

DOROTHY BEZEMES

HOMEMADE TARAMOSALATA

This delicacy was introduced to me when I first came to Chicago from Greece. I had come across this recipe while dining at a Greek restaurant in Greektown. I loved it so much that I had to make it myself. I called my aunt, Violeta, and she gave me her recipe. Whoever tries it immediately requests this recipe. It is a great dish during the fasting days of Lent or all year round during special occasions. Enjoy!

INGREDIENTS

1 – 10 oz. jar Tarama
4 medium-sized Idaho potatoes
Juice of 6 fresh lemons

2 Italian Vienna bread loaves
1/2 medium white onion
3 cups Mazola oil

Grate onion finely in a blender and boil potatoes until soft. Using a hand mixer, beat Tarama with only 3/4 cup Mazola oil. Discard ends of bread loaves approximately four inches from both sides. Slice the remaining bread approximately two inches thick and trim the crust edges. Place slices in bowl of water for about three minutes. Squeeze to remove water from saturated slices. Piece by piece, slowly add moist bread into the Tarama mixture and beat well.

Mash potatoes then slowly add to Tarama mixture and beat well. While continuing to mix, add lemon juice and remaining Mazola oil, beating between intervals. Add diced onion and mix well.

Serve as an appetizer and decorate with Greek olives. Spread on crusty bread. Serves up to 40 small appetizer portions. Another option is to make the recipe using half the Tarama jar and half of the ingredients.

CHRISTINA HIOTIS

GORTINIAN CHICKEN

In our village of Doxas Gortinias, Greece, my mother Krinio Thia Vasiloyianou, made this dish on Sundays as well as special occasions. She was quite a cook, and my father would invite people from surrounding villages to partake of her food. This one was our family favorite. It's well known in the province of Gortinia, which is located in Arcadia. Hearty and delicious, it can be served all year round.

INGREDIENTS

1 whole chicken (cut into 8 pieces)	*2 bay leaves*
1/2 cup Greek olive oil	*1 cinnamon stick*
1 large white onion (or 2 medium)	*As needed: Myzithra (or Romano)*
Dash of salt	*shredded*
Dash of pepper	*1 1/2 cups (12 oz.) tomato sauce*
2 whole eggs, beaten	*2 cups water*

Dice onion and, in a large pot, sauté in olive oil. Add salt, pepper, bay leaves, cinnamon, and tomato sauce. Cook for 10 minutes. Add chicken, and sauté for 3 minutes, turning occasionally. Add water and cook slowly for 1 hour to 1-1/2 hours. Add more water, if needed. Sauce should be thick after cooking. Remove from oven and transfer chicken to a serving platter.

Take one cup of sauce from the pot and let cool. Leave the remaining sauce in the pot. In a separate bowl, beat eggs and add Myzithra cheese, until the sauce thickens. It should be very thick. Add the sauce that was removed from the pot to cool. Add this mixture to the sauce cooking in the pot and bring to a boil. If it's too thick, add water. If too thin, add more Myzithra.

Suggestions: Serve sauce on the side, so guests can add as much or little as they like. Dip your bread in the sauce too! Serve with a horiatiki (Greek village) salad, Greek olives, Feta, homemade or other crusty bread, and Retsina wine.

Serves 5.

DIMITRA LOLOS

TEROPITES
(CHEESE TRIANGLES)

In a bowl, crumble Feta with a fork or potato masher and then combine with ricotta and eggs. Blend well. In a separate bowl, combine flour, milk, and baking powder, and mix thoroughly. Mixture should be thick, like pancake batter. Add to the cheese/egg mixture.

Follow package instructions for thawing phyllo. Combine melted butter and shortening. Cut phyllo pieces into strips, about 3 inches thick. One strip at a time, brush strips with butter mixture. Place one tsp. of cheese filling at the bottom of the strip, then fold the bottom right corner over the filling to form a triangle. Similar to folding a flag, fold the strip upward at right angles until you reach the end. Repeat with remaining pastry and filling, to create about 3 dozen triangles. With a toothpick, make 2 holes at the top of each triangle. Bake for 20 minutes at 350 degrees, until golden brown. Triangles freeze well, uncooked. When ready to use, bake at 350 degrees while still frozen. Bake 20 minutes or until golden brown. Yields 30 triangles.

FRANCES "FOFO" EGON

INGREDIENTS

3/4 lb. Feta cheese
1/2 lb. Ricotta cheese
3 eggs, beaten
1 tbsp. flour
1 tbsp. milk
1/2 tsp. baking powder
1 lb. commercial phyllo pastry sheets
1/2 lb. butter, melted
1 tbsp. solid shortening (Crisco)

KIOULPASTI
(ROAST LEG OF LAMB STUFFED WITH KEFALOTIRI)

I was raised in a small, poor village called Paloumba, near Tripoli, Greece. My mother, Millia Argyropoulos, would make kioulpasti very rarely since fresh meat was not always available to us. My two sisters and I would always crowd around the table for this delicious meal. Kioulpasti has been one of my favorite dishes ever since childhood. I am pleased to share this recipe which has been handed down to me from generations past.

Chop yellow onion, garlic, and mint leaves then combine. Add salt and pepper and put spice mix to the side.

Using a knife, cut one-inch slits around the entire leg of lamb. Rub spice mix into meat surface and into slits. Add pieces of Kefalotiri cheese into the slits. Lay out a sheet of parchment paper (ladoharto) on a flat surface. Position leg of lamb in center. Wrap it securely, folding the paper around the lamb, as though it were a package, tucking in both ends. Tie package with twine and place into a large roasting pan. Bake in preheated oven at 400 degrees for 2 1/2 to 3 hours. Serves 5 or 6.

JAMES ARGYROPOULOS

INGREDIENTS

1 leg of lamb (about 3-4 lbs.)
1 dry, yellow onion (medium size)
4 whole garlic cloves (large)
5 or 6 mint leaves
Salt and pepper to taste
1/2 lb. Kefalotiri cheese, cut into small pieces

HALVA

In a heavy saucepan over low heat, melt butter, and then add Farina. Stir constantly, for about 30 minutes, until golden brown. In a different saucepan, boil water and sugar, along with the cinnamon stick, to make the syrup. When it has boiled and piping hot, slowly drizzle syrup into Farina mixture, a little bit at a time, mixing well with every addition. It should sizzle. This means the Farina has been cooked well enough. Stir vigorously while you do this, so the final mixture takes on a thick consistency. It will not mold if its not thick enough.

Slowly add half & half, and stir vigorously until it is absorbed. When halva is thick enough to mold, remove from heat. Cover with a Turkish (or any heavy) towel for 15 minutes to absorb the steaming liquid from the halva. Grease a gelatin mold with mayonnaise, and then spoon mixture into the mold. Smooth with spoon and let cool.

Sauté almonds in butter until a rich brown color. Place them on a paper towel to absorb grease. Unmold the halva and place on a serving dish. Decorate with almonds. This is very rich, so serve small pieces.

Yields 21 small slices.

STACY DIACOU

INGREDIENTS

1/2 lb. butter (2 sticks)
2 cups Farina
2 cups half & half
1 pkg. slivered almonds

SYRUP:

3 cups sugar
4 cups water
1 cinnamon stick

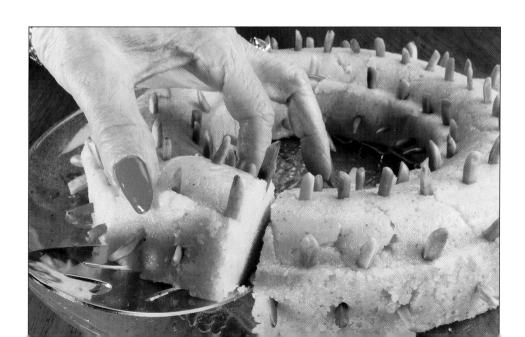

EDUCATION AND GREEK SCHOOL

From the early days of Hull House in the old Greektown neighborhood, with all of the different nationalities gathered in an adult classroom, a teacher is quoted as saying, "I think I have found the Greeks the brightest and quickest to learn." So, it is no wonder why Greek parents encouraged their offspring to focus their time and energy on education. With many of the Greeks running their own businesses, children found little time to get involved in extra-curricular activities because their available time was needed to work in the family establishment. However, the idea of children working a life-long job in the family business was not the goal. They believed a college education would open the doors of opportunity previously closed to them.

Full-time school serving residents in the old Greek Delta neighborhood began in 1908 with the formation of Socrates School. In addition, churches in the city and suburbs created after-school programs to encourage immigrant and first-generation children to preserve their culture and language.

Koraes Elementary students of Sts. Constantine & Helen Greek Orthodox Church, circa 1927. At the time, Koraes was located at 6105 South Michigan Avenue and had begun educational instruction in 1910. Today it is still thriving in Palos Hills and offers a curriculum for grades K-8, with instruction in English, Greek language, religion, and culture.

"It's a miracle when I think of it. All of our parents were uneducated. I'm talking about the guys I grew up with. They became doctors. There was a state senator. All of these people who came up from parents who didn't really have an education. But, they were hard working people and they were loving people."

"The ambition of everybody, whether they were educated or not educated, is to educate their children. Nobody says, 'I am not educated, therefore I am going to let my children be uneducated.' They always want to do more for their children than they had the opportunity to do for themselves."

"It was one of those things that we did because our parents said we had to do, but had we not done it, we would have said, 'Why didn't you force us to go to Greek school, just like you forced us to take piano lessons.'"

Pictured are students of Socrates Greek American School in 1923. Socrates Greek American School prides itself as being the oldest Greek American bilingual school in America. Established in 1908 as part of Holy Trinity Greek Orthodox Church. the academy was founded in the original Delta Greektown neighborhood. After moving several times, Socrates School will have a permanent campus in Deerfield, Illinois, in 2006, serving Kindergarten through eighth grade and offering part-time high school and adult education classes. Professor Drossos presides in the classroom scene below.

1953 class picture of Plato schoolchildren. Plato was established in 1952 as a parochial school associated with Assumption Greek Orthodox Church of Chicago. Today, Plato Academy operates as an independent school in Morton Grove. The facility serves students from Pre-K/Kindergarten through eighth grade.

Each year Greek schools from the day-school and the after-school church programs march in the Greek Independence Day parade.

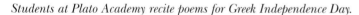

Students at Plato Academy recite poems for Greek Independence Day.

Koraes School students pose in their classroom with GreekCircle publisher, Alexa Ganakos, as part of their Media Education Day.

COMMUNITY SERVICE

After years of tireless effort by the Greek American Nursing Home Committee, and nearly five decades since the need for such a facility was identified, the Greek American Rehabilitation & Nursing Centre opened in 2001 in Wheeling.

The 204-bed Greek American Rehabilitation & Nursing Center opened in 2001. Pictured, left to right, are William Kakavas, Dr. Theodore Koutis, the mayor of Wheeling, Illinois, and John Secaras.

After WWII, the need for a facility to care for aging Greeks became apparent. In the 1950s, the Hellenic Woman's Philanthropic Association, Soteria, began raising money for this home. Their vision was for a facility that would address the physical and medical, as well as the cultural and social needs of its residents. Soteria donated their entire treasury. Many other donations followed. To date, the largest donation by an individual was made by Dr. Mary Dochios Kamberos, and by an association–the Greek American Restaurant Association (GARA). The center offers rehabilitation services, including physical and occupational therapy, treats Alzheimer's and other forms of dementia, and hospice care is also available.

In the early 1950s, the late Fr. George Mastrantonis, at left, envisioned an organization that would care for members of the Greek American community. In 1953, he and a group of civic-minded and caring community leaders founded the Hellenic Foundation.

Their first mission was to concentrate on the housing needs of the elderly, which was achieved with the purchase of Hollywood House in 1973. With the realization that individuals and families needed other social services, the Foundation created the Hellenic Family and Community Services (1975) and Hellenic Golden Circle (1979).

Hollywood House, a senior residence across the street from St. Andrew's Greek Orthodox Church, is adjacent Chicago's beautiful lakefront.

ATHLETICS

For years, basketball was the organized sport that attracted Greeks to athletic arenas. Church leagues complete with cheerleading squads and organizations like the National Hellenic Invitational Basketball Tournament, the oldest ethnic sports tournament in the U.S., have combined sport and philanthropy to raise money for important Hellenic causes. NHIBT was founded in 1931 by Phil Collias, Connie Pappas, and Dom Deliaginnis and is currently directed by Phil Bouzeos. During the early years, the NHIBT hosted many dances at the Greek-owned Aragon or Trianon ballrooms to help raise money for the tournament.

Taking part in the organized Greek basketball leagues was an important part of socializing for first-generation youth.

Greek Olympic Athletic Club—"This is an athletic club of Greek Young Men. They have exclusive use of a room for club purposes and it contains the trophies of many victories. The club was organized in November 1914, uniting two Greek Clubs, the Hercules and the Greek American."

— Hull House Year Book 1921

Kirk Vidas, former Panathinaikos Division 1 player in Greece, now plays with an NHIBT team.

Pictured are the Centaurs, an early Hull House league team.

Besides basketball Greeks excelled in other amateur and professional sports.

Born Chris Theophelos, Jim Londos was one of the all-time great wrestlers. He held the world professional title for 14 years beginning in 1930. Jim received the Gold Cross of Phoenix from King Paul of Greece.

Chris Chelios played with the Chicago Blackhawks Hockey Team for eight seasons beginning in 1990-91 and is a three-time Stanley cup champion.

"We were building this church at 71st and Stony Island, St. Constantine Church, but we were in the basement and we didn't have enough money to build the top part. So, among other [fund-raising] things we did, some guy came up with the idea to rent the old Chicago Stadium. We found an Italian Catholic parish who was also trying to build a church so we got together to have a wrestling match between Jim Londos and an Italian boxer by the name of Primo Canero. Now, you got to remember that this was 1946, right after the war, and there was no love loss between Italian Catholics and Greek Orthodox because the Italians had invaded Greece in the forties. So, I remember going by streetcar with my dad and I said, 'Dad, you know, if an Italian wins, the Greeks will go crazy, and if a Greek wins, the Italians will. This could be a riot.' He said, 'Yeah, boy, we got to watch ourselves.' So, we go into the stadium and half of it is filled with Italians and half of it with Greeks. And, they went on [wrestling] for one whole hour and they called it a draw. Thank God. It could have been a riot."

A control pitching specialist, Milt Pappas won 209 games, started the 1962 All-Star game, and threw a no hitter for the Cubs in 1972. His performances with the Cubs earned him the title the "Wrigley Field Wonder."

ON THE HOME FRONT

Presbytera Stella Christoulakis Petrakis, who received the Immigrants Service League's Distinguished Achievement Award, was a volunteer for the Red Cross for over 60 years and organized units in Chicago and across the country.

The women in this circa-1927 photo are members of the St. Helen's Benevolent Society of Sts. Constantine & Helen Church. Their president, Presbytera Petrakis, is on the right. The society assisted in the sale of "forget-me-nots" for the Edward Hines, Jr. Chapter of the Disabled American Veterans of World War I.

"We had a surplus center at Madison and Peoria where we packed clothing for people and sent them to Greece."

Children of Koraes School lend their support to the war relief effort.

There was great effort and urgency in America for the Greek War Relief effort because so many had relatives suffering in Nazi-occupied Greece during WWII. Reverend Mark Petrakis, far left; Presbytera Petrakis, far right; and church sexton, Spiro Georgelas, on far right packing a box, are joined by the women of Sts. Constantine & Helen Greek Orthodox Church at 6105 South Michigan as they ship clothing to Greece.

IN THEIR HONOR

When America entered World War I, there was not a more loyal and patriotic class of people in the country than the American Greeks. An estimated one out of four Greeks (some 60,000) served in the Great War—a percentage higher than any other ethnic group. In this war and others that came later, Greek Americans were proud to represent their adopted country. They served in all capacities—from cooks to captains. Moreover, these heroes never forgot their Greek roots and willingly answered the call to go back and fight for their homeland during the Balkan Wars of 1912-1913.

Serving in WWI, George Tountas in 1918.

"Things did happen, too gruesome to talk about. I had a good time in the service, like when I spent one year in Paris. So, along with all the bad times in the service, I had good memories. But, all in all, it was an experience I would not want to repeat—yet, I wouldn't give it up for anything! It was something I'm glad I experienced, and I hope nobody else has to."

Themistocles Godelas in 1917-1918 serving in the Infantry.

"I knew everyone else was being drafted, being inducted into the army, and it was just one of those things that we had to do. And, it was a patriotic thing to do, so I went right along with it."

"WWII was bad because my brothers were both in it, and then my husband was in it. And, many of the boys I grew up with were in it. I was writing to three or four boys that we knew. They were about my age. And, there was sugar rationing, butter rationing—all that kind of stuff that you had to watch out for."

Gregory Ganakos, serving in WWI, was honored in this patriotic discharge photo.

Peter Kapsalis plays the violin to entertain his comrades in the military.

Gus Kay (Katsikas), WWII Navy veteran, is a survivor of the famous USS Indianapolis *that sank in the Pacific on July 30, 1945 after being torpedoed. He is one of 7 of 129 that survived 5 days in the water, and overall 1 of 317 of 1,197 men that survived from the entire ship.*

Sam Maragos, WWII.

Naval Third Class Seaman, George A. Svourakis.

Family welcomes home Nick Ganakos serving in WWII.

"Until now, we knew that Greeks were fighting like heroes; from now on we shall say that the heroes fight like Greeks."
           —*Winston Churchill*

"I'm very proud to be Greek, and of the Greek people. {They} are very energetic and if they have a cause, they'll fight till the end for it."

"Let every man honor and love the land of his birth, and the race from which he springs, and keep their memory green. It is a pious and honorable duty, but let us all be Americans."
           —*Henry Cabot Lodge*

Tom Mallers plays cards with an army buddy.

John Secaras in his dress whites.

Corporal John J. Stamos serving in the spring of 1945 in Belgium.

"My dad served in the Greek army and one month after the bombing of Pearl Harbor, I enlisted in the army. My dad didn't want me to go, but I reminded him, 'You went back to serve in the country that you were born in, so now I want to serve in the country that I was born in.'" Andrew Athens, at left in vehicle, served as an Army Captain in WWII and a liaison officer with the Belgian Government. After the military, he became founding President of Metron Steel Corporation.

Daniel Simopoulos, at age 22, served in the Korean War.

"I spent three years in the service and then came out and went to the University of Illinois. This was paid for by the G.I. Bill of Rights which was given to the WWII veterans."

Georgia Demitralis stands proud with her two sons, Spiro Demitralis of the WWII D-Day 82nd Airborne Division and George Demitralis of the WWII D-Day 2nd Infantry.

Greek immigrant, George Dilboy, is honored with a statue on the grounds of the Hines Veterans Hospital. He arrived in America at age 17 and at age 21, he was called into service. That same year, 1918, he was killed on the battlefield in France. He was posthumously awarded the Congressional Medal for Bravery, the highest medal of the Republic. He was the first Greek to receive this honor.

LIFE AS A GREEK AMERICAN

. After the initial struggles of adjusting to life in America, Greeks began the delicate balancing act of maintaining their ethnic traditions while blending in with American society. Marriage formed the basis for a strong family foundation, and maintaining a good home environment was a priority. As the extended family grew, generations of Greek Americans, like the symbolic "koufetta" candy, enjoyed the sweetness and bitterness of life. Events of family, friends, and the various church and Hellenic organizations always kept the Greeks close to their cultural roots and gave them the strength to achieve great success here in America.

Yiayia Margaret and Papou George Thodoropoulos relaxing inside their home at 1224 North Washtenaw in the Humboldt Park area of Chicago in the 1950s.

The wedding of George and Mary (Koutselas) Alpogianis in 1922.

Anitsa and Louis Malleris relax in the park outside of the Edgewater Beach Hotel on the city's North Side in the 1930s.

Katina Paptsoris is pictured with two of her 19 grandchildren, Mary (Dalianis) Aravosis and George Dalianis, in 1936 in Greece. Katina lived in Messinia in Peloponnesus, and with her husband, George, raised seven children. She lived through two wars, during which she lost one son, and wore black till her death at age 94. Some of her grandchildren remained in Greece, but the majority immigrated to the United States, Germany, Brazil, and Panama.

"Today's no different from the old days. A lot of widows still wear black for the rest of their life."

"I think that everyone pitches in and does their share. Families strive and work, and they have a common goal. And, if the wife has to work, you all pitch in, and that's what we did. We all pitched in and made things happen, made things work."

A group of women who lived and operated businesses with their husbands near Hull House in Greektown enjoy a day at Mrs. Eliopoulos' home (the Greek music store owner's), in Maywood. Standing, left to right, are Dora Mavridou, Mercina Lagouros, Edna Galanopoulos, and Esthemia Godelas. Seated, left to right, are Mrs. Eliopoulos, hostess, and Mrs. Kanellopoulos.

In front of Estelle's Food Shop near Addison Street and Oak Park Avenue in the early 1960s. Left to right, Evgenia Pappas, Estelle Palmos, Fotini Terzis.

Al Sofiakis and Angela Nikoletseas Sofiakis and their first-born daughter, Marianthe. This is in 1954 in the yard of their home on Waveland in Chicago.

"We were part of the Greek community. Because of our church, we would go to school for Greek, and go to church for Sunday School. It was our social life. But, that was our life. It was the church, it was our friends and everything Greek."

John Kouchoukos sits on the backsteps with his three boys—Frank at his knees, George, and James, the baby. John worked as a shoe cobbler. Frank was born deaf so the family, for his benefit, learned to sign.

Standing outside St. George Greek Orthodox Church on Sheffield near Diversey Avenue in Chicago, circa 1956, are newlyweds Angie and George Callas joined by niece and nephew Patricia and Mark Mellonas.

"Socially, the Greeks that came from Greece they would stay with their group over here, because they became friendly and they would have parties and meet every so often and then they would do things to help their people in Greece. If they made money here, they would put money together and send it back for different things in their villages."

John Geavaras immigrated in 1903 and Bertha Geavaras arrived in 1916. In the photo above, they are married at Holy Trinity Greek Orthodox Church on February 11, 1917. Father Pegeas and all in attendance are captured in a formal family photo in front of the altar in honor of the marriage sacrament performed.

The baptism of Constantine Psichogios in 1922. Standing, left to right, Bertha Psichogios, Peter Psichogios, baby Constantine, George Philosophos, and Ifigenia Philosophos. Children in front, left to right, Louis Philosophos, Carrie Philosophos, Connie Philosophos, and Theresa Philosophos.

"Coming over at the age of 7, not knowing the language, you had a little handicap. But, that was not a problem. The children communicate even if the language is not a common bridge between them, and it didn't take us long to learn the language. We started out as immigrants, but ended up as bonafide American citizens."

This charming photograph not only served as a family keepsake but also a treasure to be sent back to Yiayia and Papou in the "old country."

Adrienne Parrish Papadakos in 1944 at her home on Chicago Avenue and Hamlin.

Demetra Lalagos, the daughter of Demetrios (James) Lalagos, in 1955 on the bar at the Acropolis Restaurant and Tavern which was a thriving business in the center of Greektown on Blue Island Avenue. James also owned a grocery store which ran a successful import business.

"Everyone that goes to Greek school has to learn poems for the 25th of March, the Greek Independence Day. And my grandmothers were entrusted with teaching those poems, so the day the performance came, they were perfect."

Dressing in traditional Greek costumes at Socrates School was a joy for both youngsters and proud parents.

"Greek was the language we spoke in our homes. In fact, until our parents died, we only spoke to them in Greek. It was just a natural thing to do, and we never thought about it. You would speak English to one group and turn around and speak Greek to the other one."

Helen and Louis Graves stand in front of their home in the 1940s.

"We see those fancy scooters that the young kids have today–we used to make them out of a 2' x 4' and a pair of roller skates and an orange crate. And,[we] would fly a kite once in a while, get in a disagreement and throw a few stones at each other–and the next thing you would go out and have ice cream together."

Spero Melonides is held by his mother, Panagiota, during a portrait sitting in Chicago in the 1930s.

"There was actually two societies. There was the Greek society and then there were the fellows I went to high school with and played ball with. You lived in two worlds. You straddled both sides. But, we weren't the only ones because in the neighborhood where I grew up, there were a lot of Italian families and Polish families and they did the same thing. We sort of empathized with everyone else."

Gregory G. Ganakos enjoying a ride in his toy car on Bishop Street on the South Side.

*Joining in on Easter Day, circa 1945,
Katherine Frankos, Angie Pappas, and
Angeline Frankos enjoy the view from their
home on 946 West Schubert behind St. George
Greek Orthodox Church.*

*The Koumbari cousins enjoy a beach vacation together in New Buffalo, Michigan, circa,
1939. Berrien County was such a popular vacation spot for Chicago Greeks escaping life
in the fast-paced city. "Every summer, year after year after year, the Greeks of Chicago
returned to their beloved summer cottages or resort communities to recreate a "micro-
Greece"—speaking the Greek language, grilling lamb as well as hotdogs and hamburgers,
singing Greek songs, and dancing the Greek circle dances around the campfires."*

"It's just the Greek culture. Everything revolves
around the church. Even when you are not at the
church, the socialization that goes on in different
homes are with people from the church. It's sort of
like how people say, 'I'm from the north side,
south side, east side. Well Greeks do the same
thing: 'I'm from St. Andrew's.' 'Oh, North-sider.'
Or, 'I'm from St. Nick's.' 'Oh, you're a South-
sider.' So, it's your geography."

*Magda Simopoulos and Angelo Tsarpalas on a date for the Wells
High School Senior Prom on Saturday, June 5, 1954.*

A very typical Greek scene. "Of course, in Greektown, you would stop at the coffee houses, which were probably for men only. Women wouldn't go there. But for the young people like myself, we knew a lot of the old-timers. They talk to you. Tell you stories about coming over from there to here—what they went through. A lot of them were bachelors who never got married so they spent a lot of time in the neighborhood coffee house."

"Those meals that we spent together, all of the family, the extended family together, I can't think of happier times. Because we just laughed. There was no kids' table. All the kids sat at the same table as the adults. So, it was a really big table."

James Lalagos, at right back, of the Acropolis Restaurant and Tavern, and his one-time partner, Angelo Pappas, seated at right, are photographed in the early 1940s. James and his family lived in a modest apartment above the store on Blue Island Avenue and owned the entire city block. Many of those neighboring storefronts were places where he would set up newly arrived immigrants into business. Originally from Tegeas, Greece, he personally sponsored about 1,000 Greeks from the Arcadia region to come to America. He also helped them to find jobs, housing, and fed many families during the Depression.

A 1950s Sunday party with the Themi and Stavroula Papadakos family.

Elias Rombakis and his sister, Evyenia, in the backyard at the 3569 South Archer Avenue residence that Elias shared with another sister, Georgia Kriaris. The house was fondly called the Kriaris Hotel by the many Greek immigrants who made it their temporary home.

"From the top of the stairs, we could hear the sounds of the festive Greek music serenading us from the apartment door. We'd walk through the door and smell all of the foods that would be awaiting us from that banquet feast that Thea had been preparing for days for Theo's nameday."

Christ Thodoropoulos, at right, and cousin, Elias, sport the trendy American styles of the era. Christ immigrated to America in 1930, attended adult education classes at Hull House, worked as a dishwasher for $8 a week, and eventually was the successful owner of many movie theaters in Chicago.

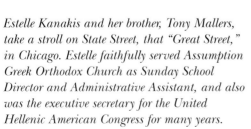

Estelle Kanakis and her brother, Tony Mallers, take a stroll on State Street, that "Great Street," in Chicago. Estelle faithfully served Assumption Greek Orthodox Church as Sunday School Director and Administrative Assistant, and also was the executive secretary for the United Hellenic American Congress for many years.

Angeline Frankos standing in front of her fiancé's (George Callas) car at his godfather's house in Antioch, Illinois, circa 1950.

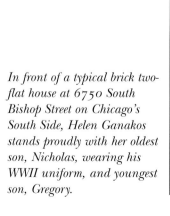

In front of a typical brick two-flat house at 6750 South Bishop Street on Chicago's South Side, Helen Ganakos stands proudly with her oldest son, Nicholas, wearing his WWII uniform, and youngest son, Gregory.

Helen Kanakis and Estelle Kanakis enjoy a visit from their son and brother, respectively, Anthony Mallers, serving in the U.S. Army.

"And, in the process of life, I met many Greek families. I chose each and every one of them. They had to be hard working, and have morals and ethics. They had to be the salt of the earth people. And, that is how I spent my life with friends. And, of course, I was going to the Assumption Church on Harrison and Central. When you go to church, it's like going home. The one you left behind."

THE WEDDING

The marriage of Jim and Katy Demetriades in 1921. As few people had cars in the 1920s, the wedding, the dinner, and dance reception were held in the same public venue, whether indoors or outdoors.

Through marriage, an extended family is formed with the koumbara *(best man), who is usually a friend or relative from outside the immediate family, and later serves as godfather to the couple's first child.*

"My uncle decided that this was the man for my mother. So my uncle brought my father to my mother and said, 'This is your husband, this is the man you will marry.'"

One of the first Greek Orthodox weddings in Chicago was celebrated in 1916. Many times picnic groves were used for the reception festivities.

The Greeks have a rich tradition of embroidered, sewn, and hand-woven textiles that served as an integral part in daily life as furnishings for the home, as well as the celebration of marriage. Most of the textiles were brought to this country from Greece. Created prior to 1950, they offer insight into the traditions that Greek immigrants treasured when they came to the United States.

Gus and Sophie Malevitis in 1927 after their wedding celebration at Sts. Constantine & Helen Greek Orthodox Church.

Many brides today remember their roots by returning to their homeland to host their marriage. Melissa Ganakos takes the traditional donkey ride through the village on her wedding day in May 2001, to meet her fiancé, Chris Poindexter, who is waiting at the church.

The bridesmaid attendants of Chris and Claire George after their marriage at Sts. Constantine & Helen Greek Orthodox Church in 1946.

THE LOVE OF DANCE

"The music leads us to the dance floor with friends and relatives, young and old, and we join hands to form a line which links us to our ancestors. Greek dancing is more than just something we do at weddings, it is a piece of our culture that reaches deep inside our history."

The authenticity of dance and costumes is something that many dance troupes are trying to preserve. Besides individual church dance troupes, there have been more than a dozen troupes in the Chicago area including the Agape, Apollo, Cretan, Macedonian, Olympian, and Orpheus. These troupes keep this important tradition alive.

Greeks dance at Hull House in 1951 as part of a carnival celebration.

"We all remember our father teaching us, lining up to teach us the Lord's Prayer in Greek which we never forgot. And, he'd pay us to sing, to dance Greek, I remember he'd give us a quarter. We held it when we were in front of the line and I remember never keeping it, but never being unhappy 'cause he gave it to the next one to dance. So, we all knew how to dance Greek."

Dr. Mary Dochios Kamberos, generous contributor of both the Greek American Rehabilitation& Nursing Centre and the Hellenic Museum and Cultural Center, leads a dance.

Enjoying a dance at the wedding of Mary and William Kyriazis in 1953.

Kicking up their heels at the wedding of Ben and Penny (Katehos) Renda in 1963 with Tom Thodoropoulos leading, followed by Louie Papadakos, Penny Renda, Ben Renda, Adrienne Parrish, Pat Katehos, and Alex Katehos.

The Cretan Club joins together at a group event at Hull House, circa 1928.

Presbytera Petrakis, at right in photo with black coat, directed a dance group that performed at functions throughout Chicago.

"What we do is expose the next generation of Greeks to a huge part of their culture–how beautiful, rich, and meaningful every part of it is. The troupe uses colorful costumes representing different regions of Greece, from the long, black, pleated skirts and silver buckles of Asia Minor to the flowery, vibrant, feminine dresses of the Ionian Islands. Each has historical or cultural significance."

The Olympian Dance Troupe warms up before a performance on Halsted Street. The president of Greece, Costis Stephanopoulos, joined His Eminence Metropolitan Iakovos and Mayor Richard M. Daley to inaugurate the newly refurbished Greektown in May 1996. The Olympian Dance Troupe has been dancing since 1988.

The Orpheus Hellenic Dance Group entertain attendees of the 100th anniversary party of the Greek Star newspaper in 2004. This troupe began in 1989.

Members of the dance troupe at St. Sophia Greek Orthodox Church perform at their annual festival in Elgin, Illinois.

GREEK WOMEN'S GROUPS

As more women immigrated to the United States they formed clubs and associations to aid in their assimilation to this country. They put their energy and leadership skills to work to plan activities for the Greek American society—including many charitable efforts.

"Twenty years ago Greek mothers of the neighborhood had an active Club which met at Hull House. Last year the Club, which had dwindled away, began meeting again. They elected Mrs. Koulla Konomidas president. Thursday night was Mrs. Konomidas' first appearance in the role of club president. Apparently she was born for the part. One seldom sees a leader possessing such animation, reticence, and poise all at one time." [18]

Women have been the backbone of many Greek families and also found the time to organize clubs and activities for the community.

The Gold Star Mothers aided Greek men in the army with their outreach efforts. One soldier wrote: "It was the best Christmas gift I received. If only I could explain to you what that little gift does to the morale of the Greek boys in the army. It isn't the gift so much as it is the idea that the Greek people back home are thinking of us." This group met in Sts. Constantine & Helen's multi-purpose room which was part of the church's extensive complex at 6105 South Michigan Avenue and was built after the church fire in 1926.

A group of ladies visit with Miss Greece, Ms. Aliki Diplaraka, at the home of Dr. and Mrs. S.D. Soter in Chicago in 1931.

Participating in organized teas and luncheons were a big part of socializing for Greek women.

The Cretan Ladies Fraternity, Amalthia, was formed by Presbytera Petrakis, center seated. This group met regularly to aid in philanthropy efforts for the island of Crete, assist Cretans now living in the United States, and to preserve the traditions of their island homeland.

Members of the Greek Women's University Club formed in 1931 to encourage philanthropic, cultural, and educational activities for women. Standing, from left to right, are Barbara Petrakis Manta, Ellie Lambrakis, Sophia Diamant, Mary Maniaty Spanon, and Ione Kosmetos Soter. Venette Askounes, seated, worked for the Immigrant Protective League for 30 years and was instrumental in aiding immigrants to adjust to their new lives in the United States. She also was a Koraes schoolteacher.

Members of the Young Ladies Philomusical Hellenic Society pose for a group photo in 1954.

Members of the St. Andrew's Philoptochos Society gather around the kitchen table to finalize last-minute details for an event they are hosting.

Philoptochos-sponsored luncheons by various churches, as well as the Chicago Diocesan Philoptochos Board, have been a successful part of the fundraising efforts for this philanthropic woman's organization.

ROASTING LAMB

When it comes to a meat dish, lamb is the traditional choice for most Greeks. This early Chicago newspaper, recounts the joy of lamb roasting with the celebration of Easter:

"Nowhere in Chicago was Easter celebrated with more gaiety than in the Greek colony centering at Blue Island Avenue and Halsted Street. The coffee shops were decorated with rosettes and gonfalons and banners proclaiming *Kalo Pascha* or Happy Easter.

The fragrance of barbecued lamb rose from the charcoal pits along Blue Island Avenue, where entire carcasses were wrapped up for family dinners.

But nowhere in the colony was the holiday more observed more festively than the home of Tom Janapoulos, 848 Vernon Park Place. At 8 o'clock in the morning the charcoal pits in Tom's backyard were lighted, and for six hours Tom's children, nephews, and nieces slowly turned the lambs on spits.

At 2 o'clock Tom and his family, his three brothers and their families, friends and relatives, 35 in all, sat down to their annual Easter feast. Uncle Angelo Soprano and Uncle George Veisslokia were there, as was Petros Makropolos, editor of a Greek newspaper.

The Paschal lamb was washed down by plenty of Greek wine."

"At Easter time, Greeks came from all over Chicago to purchase their lambs from Lalagos. It is quite legendary among the older generations about their trips to Greektown to buy lamb. James and his associates would set up spits in all the backyards on the street. Patrons would come on Easter, after church, to select a lamb. Sometimes they would stay. This ritual became quite a celebration. The older folks, as well as the kids, would take a hand at turning the spit. The music would play, the dancing would commence, and the wine would flow." [19]

Gus and Paul Kalpake and Gus Alpogianis, in the comfort of their backyard and using modern technology, still enjoy the traditional Easter lamb roasting in 1992.

At major celebration times like Easter, spits were set up in the back alleys of Chicago to roast several lambs and enjoy each other's company. Circa 1930.

PICNICS AND FESTIVALS

In the early 1900s, picnics and outings played a dominant role in the social life of immigrant Greeks. These Greek-only affairs, which began simply and modestly with a small gathering of friends and relatives in someone's backyard or in a picnic grove, were a way to be outdoors, eat delicious homemade food, and enjoy one another's company. Business deals were made, marriages were arranged, and new political frontiers were explored. It was a time when summer nights with family, food, friends, and conversation were all anyone needed to feel contented.

The first Greek picnics were sponsored by organizations from various parts of Greece, such as the Laconian Society, the Messinian Society, the Paleohoritans, and many others that provided a taste of Greece for Greek American citizens. The Assumption Church on Central and Harrison in Chicago was among the first to host a picnic, and this church, and many others that followed, used the picnic to generate additional income for the congregation.

During the '50s and '60s, the Greek picnic evolved into "Hellenic Festivals" —huge fundraising events held at local churches designed not only to help raise money but also to coalesce the Greek community. In the 1950s, life was more reserved, so even in 90-degree weather, everyone—even children—was expected to dress as though they were going to church…because they were. Every man wore a suit and tie; all the women donned their finest dresses and hats. Men shined their shoes while women had their hair done.

Besides a special social event, these picnics provided needed funds to build and renovate churches, support the parish, and fund philanthropic outreach. Picnics today, like yesteryear, fill social calendars each summer and provide an opportunity to visit with family and friends belonging to different church communities. Greeks, and non-Greeks alike, look forward each year to their favorite Greek festivals to enjoy the sounds of Greek music, the smell of souvlaki, and the chance to create more sweet summer memories!

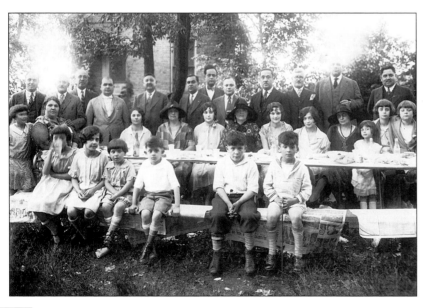

Sts. Constantine & Helen family picnic, circa 1915.

St. Demetrios Greek Orthodox Church of Elmhurst, Illinois, hosts one of the largest picnics in the Chicago area—complete with carnival attractions for the family.

"When my brother, sister, and I were very young, one of the highlights of our lives was when Dad and Mom used to take us to the Messinian Society Picnic every summer. The family would get on the Ashland streetcar for 7 cents and go north to Irving Park Road and then travel west until the end of the streetcar line. We kids would all run to be the first on the streetcar, so we could stand next to the motorman and the wind would rush across our faces as the streetcar moved forward. After an hour ride, we'd reach the picnic grove. The Greek music got louder and louder as we got closer and closer to the grove. The smell of souvlaki, chicken, and smelt would fill the air. While waiting for Dad to buy the food, we would all go to the dance floor and do the *syrto*, the *tsamiko*, and the *hasposerviko*, with all our friends and relatives. Dad returned with several plates of souvlakia, Greek bread, and tomatoes. Coke (and wine for the adults) helped to wash down the excellent food. More dancing followed until it was time to go home. By the end of the day, we kids were tired and fell asleep on the long ride home. That night we thought we couldn't wait until next year when once again we'd go to the Messinian Picnic at the Jolly Grove. Aah, sweet memories!   *Ernie Neokos*

Village fraternity members in 1925 celebrate with the smell of lamb roasting in the air.

"Did we dress up for picnics? You bet we did. I used to take pony rides in a three-piece suit at the Assumption Picnic in Pilsen Park in the summer of 1956. I remember the first time I saw a man without a tie–I was traumatized."

Family and extended family members gather for a photo in an outdoor picnic setting, circa 1920s.

Family outing of the members of the Scopenon and Elpis societies in July 1928.

"The costumes are as important as the dancing itself. For example, in the costume from Macedonia, the women wear a headpiece that looks like a helmet. It reminds us of the wars Alexander the Great led and how the brave women put on their dead husbands' helmets and persevered. It's a symbol of strength and of hard-fought freedom."

Eustathia Panousis, of the Olympian Greek Dance Troupe, models a Karagouna *costume, originating from the mountainous regions of Thessaly in Northern Greece.* Kara *in Turkish, means black, and* gouni *means turban. Thus, the name of the costume symbolizes the black turbans the women wore on their heads during the Turkish occupation. Additionally, the costume encompasses seven layers, as it can get very cold in the mountains.*

No festival is complete without a performance from a Greek dance troupe. Wearing costumes from the many regions of Greece, dancers perform traditional dances from throughout Greece and the islands. Greeks and Greeks-for-a-day, enjoy a performance by the Olympian Greek Dance Troupe, at St. Andrew's festival, on Chicago's North Side.

*The ladies of the Olympian Greek Dance Troupe perform in traditional costumes. From left, are costumes from Macedonia, the northern most region of Greece (*Makedonissa*); Thessaly, in Northern Greece (*Karagouna*); the island of Corfu (*Kerkera*), Asia Minor (*Sarakatsana—a nomadic group of Greeks who originated in Asia Minor*) and Western Thrace (*Metaxades*). The dancers are, left to right, Susan Downs, Eustathia Panousis, Connie Kapos, Jenny Stavropoulos, and Andrea Zurales.*

From the savory souvlaki or shishkebob dinner, bottom right, served in a white foam carton, to the traditional gyros sandwich, top left, made of a mixture of pressed lamb and beef served with grilled pita bread, top right, there is no chance a stomach will ever go away hungry at a Greek festival. The popular gyros sandwich finds its roots in Chicago as it remains home to all major gyros manufacturers like Grecian Delight, Corfu Foods, Olympia Foods, and Kronos Products of which founder Chris Tomaras, in 1975, discovered a need to create a processed uniform gyros product that could provide consistency in taste. Besides a delicious dinner, one needs to save room for the traditional Greek pastries, bottom left, that the women of the church have been preparing for days and weeks. In addition to the famous baklava, galaktobouriko, kourambiedes, and a plate of the honey-drenched and cinnamon-sprinkled loukoumades are the best treats for sharing with friends and family on a warm summer night.

THE HELLENIC DEBUTANTE COTILLION

Since its inception in 1965, more than 2,500 debutantes and escorts have been presented at this gala gathering which is one of the highlights of the social season and has raised over $3,000,000 for philanthropic causes.

Emerging out of the established Celestial Soiree sponsored by the Women's Club of Sts. Constantine & Helen Greek Orthodox Church, the Hellenic Debutante Cotillion was a community event to introduce young Hellenic ladies to adult society and perpetuate Greek culture, heritage, and philanthropic endeavors. This time-honored tradition served as a fund-raiser for the church, philoptochos, and select charities.

The first cotillion premiered in 1965 and provided a venue for debutantes and escorts to meet each other, not only at the Ball, but also at various pre-parties hosted by Greek-American families throughout the year. The Hellenic Debutante Cotillion was enjoyed for 30 years and then revived by eight former debutantes in 1998 to give their sons and daughters a similar social experience. The Hellenic League now sponsors the Debutante Cotillion & Crystal Ball to carry on this elegant tradition.

A debutante, escorted by her father, bows to the Bishop, symbolizing her introduction into the community as an adult.

THE PARADE

From the first parade in 1965, the annual Greek Independence Day parade has become an event of pomp, pageantry, and fun. But its meaning and purpose is much more serious and dramatic.

In 1453, our ancestors, the Hellenes, were taken over by the Turks. This period in Greece's history was undoubtedly the toughest and most oppressive. During the time of the Ottoman occupation, there were no schools nor religion. Churches and icons had been destroyed. But the Greeks' love of education and learning sparked the creation of the *krifo scolio*, the hidden school, which taught children the Greek language and the Orthodox religion. However, it was their proud history, powerful sense of culture, and compelling desire to be free that led the Greeks to overthrow the Ottoman occupation and proclaim victory. On March 25th, 1821 (400 years later), the Ottoman Turk occupation finally ceased.

This is what is celebrated on those warm days on Michigan Avenue or Halsted Street.

Dignitaries join for the start of the Greek Heritage Parade down Michigan Avenue. For many years beginning in 1975, this parade was organized by the United Hellenic American Congress (UHAC) but currently is hosted by ENOSIS, a federation uniting many Greek organizations. The route runs down Halsted Street in Chicago's Greektown neighborhood.

Mayor Richard M. Daley, third from left, is joined by Governor George Ryan, fifth from left, as Greek Americans march down State Street for the annual Greek Independence Day parade. It is felt that March 25 celebrates a commitment to freedom and to democracy that is shared by Greece and America.

"The parade itself honors the spirit and people who fought for freedom from 400 years of oppression. This simple marching down the street pays tribute to the struggle our ancestors endured from difficulties we cannot even imagine."

Greek dancers perform in Daley Plaza as part of the events of Greek Heritage Week—leading up to the parade.

The Annunciation Cathedral and St. Demetrios Church of Chicago share a float honoring 500 years of Greek theatre. For years, these two churches were connected through the Solon Greek School which served the needs of the youth in the development of their Greek language skills.

The precision movement of the Evzones, *symbolic of the Greek Royal Palace Guard, graces the parade route. The white skirt,* foustanella, *is made from over 30 yards of material, pressed into 400 pleats, representing the 400 years of the Turkish occupation.*

Members of the Macedonian Society march down State Street in tradi-tional costumes. As one of many organizations to march each year in the parade, the Society exemplifies pride of their regional roots.

The blue and white colors of the Greek flag symbolize the blue of the sea and the white of the waves. The nine stripes are based on the number of syllables in the Greek phrase: Eleutheia H Thanatos (Freedom or Death) which was the motto during the revolution against the Ottoman Empire. And, the cross in the corner symbolizes the honor the people demonstrate to the church and Christianity.

Greek Americans gather at Daley Plaza to watch the raising of the Greek flag in honor of Greek Independence Day.

Every parade needs spectators to wave flags at floats and marchers along the parade route.

Before floats graced the streets of Michigan Avenue, State Street, and then Halsted Street, Greek Independence Day was celebrated in large venues, like the Medinah Temple, where several thousand Greeks packed the auditorium to watch singers and dance troupes perform, and listen to poems and speeches celebrating Greece's triumphant victory and hard-won independence.

Floats depicting various Hellenistic ideals highlight the parade route, and they provide on-lookers with a strong sense of the passion demonstrated for various Greek causes and the organizations they represent.

"I'm marching like my papou did."

Cold, warm, rain or shine, the parade each year has brought thousands of Greeks together to march side-by-side. Before and after the parade, Greektown restaurants buzz with excitement and joyous celebration.

PUBLIC INSTALLATION OF OFFICERS
OF THE AHEPA, CHAPTERS NUMBER
46, 93, 94, & 103
ARAGON BALLROOM - CHICAGO

With over 5,500 in attendance, this was the public installation of officers of the American Hellenic Educational Progressive Association, Chapters 46, 93, 94, and 103 hosted at the famed Aragon Ballroom in Chicago on January 16, 1928. The Aragon and Trianon ballrooms were owned by Andrew and his brother, William Karzas, and were popular venues for Greek American young adults to go ballroom dancing. The AHEPA is the largest Greek American organization, with chapters in the United States, Canada, Australia, Greece and Cyprus. Formed in 1922 as a non-partisan and non-sectarian organization, it helped to bring Greek Americans together, protect them from the evils of bigotry, and aided struggling immigrants assimilate into American society.

ENTERTAINMENT

From formal banquets, to concerts and movies, to dinner in Greektown with friends–Greek Americans always make time to celebrate. They not only enjoy being entertained, but they also enjoy being the entertainer, as they excel in many creative endeavors, like music, theater, and culinary arts.

Steve and Olga Harris, owners of Club Hollywood, featured many top performers at their entertainment nightclub from 1946-1959. The beautifully appointed venue was also a very popular destination for high school Prom couples because Club Hollywood created an enticing dinner package for the school's special night.

Deni's Den filled many lives with music from 1969-1996. Originally located on Lawrence Avenue, it eventually moved to its Clark Street location. The large facility hosted private parties and concerts, and also functioned as a Greek restaurant serving food until the early morning hours. Patrons danced and threw dollars and flowers to the rhythm of live bands and talented singers–many brought in from Greece. Deni's Den was a frequent stop for visitors, including Anthony Quinn, Melina Mercouri, Mikos Theodorakis, Prime Minister Andreas Papandreou, and Jacqueline Bisset, who originally intended to stop by for five minutes, but ended staying and dancing until 5:00 a.m. According to Chris Verdos, an owner, and wife, Georgia, it was a very happy place because they helped to make sure that the customers felt like they were in the comforts of "home" enjoying savory food, music, and a festive environment.

DIANNA'S OPAA

Self proclaimed as the "Mayor of Greektown," Petros Kogiones was the popular host of Dianna's restaurant which expanded and changed locations on Halsted Street from a storefront grocery to a larger site where everyone was treated like a VIP.

Zorba the Greek comes to mind when you shake hands with Petros Kogiones, former proprietor of the famous Dianna's Opaa Restaurant on Chicago's West Side. But after experiencing him, you realize Kogiones is a man, who "has walked with kings and not lost the common touch." Petros awakened his *philoxenia* (love for strangers) in his first catering stint at the Officers Club in Greece satisfying the fastidious appetites of NATO directors and King Constantine of Greece. Not bad for an aspiring schoolteacher from the mountain village, Nestani, in Arcadia. In 1961, he arrived in Chicago hoping to study psychology but opened a 5-table café, run mainly by his brother, Pete. (His father, Big Nick, had arrived in 1907.) Dianna's Opaa premiered in 1974 where guests were known to wait two hours in zero-degree weather. Petros became the owner, the host, the showman, and Chicago's brightest star. "Welcome," he intones, "Everyone is Greek tonight."

President George H. Bush told Petros that if he cut his trademark long, wavy hair, he could come to the White House. He did and he went.

"The food was good, but the atmosphere was electric. Dianna's was the place to be."

Before leading his guests in Greek song and dance, Petros distributes hugs and handshakes, flourishes bottles of retsina as well as armloads of Greek salad.

With flash and a flourish, a cry of Opaa!, Petros flames up saganaki with Greek brandy, a cheese hors d'oeuvre, original to the world-renowned restaurant. The eyes of the guests light up like fireworks on the Fourth of July.

Anthony Quinn, cinema's Zorba, tried to imitate his host by dancing the hassapiko with a bottle of wine perched on his head, (he broke 3 bottles). Ted Kennedy, Spiro Agnew, Michael Dukakis also dropped by to be entertained.

Greeks have always had a love affair with kaffeneia, coffee houses, where Greek American men once passed myriad hours reading newspapers and discussing politics of the day.

Lou Mitchell's coffee shop has become a popular breakfast destination for all Chicagoans. In this photo-op, the well-known host of Greek ancestry, Lou Mitchell, at right, stands across the street from his famous restaurant in the Chicago Loop.

Actor Billy Zane is a Chicago native who starred in the blockbuster movie Titanic. *Sister Lisa Zane is also known for her acting career including the film* Femme Fatale *and television appearances on* Law and Order *and* ER. *Not surprising, talent runs in the family, as parents, William and Thalia Zane, are seasoned stage performers.*

George Papadatos, Vasilios Gaitanos, Vasili Rousis, and Alex Galas were members of the band and recording artists that entertained crowds at Deni's Den.

Andrea Darlas of WGN-AM Radio, second from left, greets Nia Vardelos of My Big Fat Greek Wedding *fame and her parents after an interview. The movie premiered in Chicago at an event hosted by the Hellenic Museum and Cultural Center. The opening scene of the movie set the stage as Chicago with its magnificent skyline.*

Greek Island Restaurant staff, left to right, Texas Kalotihos, George Sakis, Apostolos Bournos, Filandros Sguros, and Gus Couchell make sure the lamb roasting on the restaurant spit is just right for eager customers.

A visit by actor Anthony Quinn is reason enough for Greek Islands' Restaurant managing partner, Gus Couchell, to do the Zorba dance for customers.

Owner Manolis Mastropoulos, and Kalliope, Manolis, and Jimmy Kostatinidis stand outside the Grecian Gardens which was a popular nightclub on Halsted Street from 1955-1978. The famous Greek performers, Trio Bel Canto, had their first U.S appearance at this bouzouki.

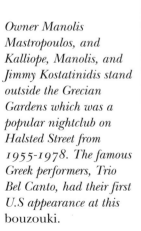

New Year's Eve 1972 is celebrated at the festive Grecian Gardens.

The Hellenic Choral Society entertained audiences in Chicago and Greece from 1981 to 1999. Georgia Mitchell, holding flowers, served as the dedicated and inspirational choir director during those years.

The Koraes School Student Orchestra with stringed instruments and piano accompaniment performed often to the delight of students, staff, and families.

Socrates School cast members pose after their magnificent performance of the classic play, Antigone, *in 2003.*

GREEK BUSINESS

To feed the onset of the Industrial Revolution, waves of immigrants arrived on U.S. soil. As the struggling, abused labor force, they fueled the railroads and the stockyards. However, some of the Greek immigrants, with their proclivity to entrepreneurship, moved beyond and above this hardship.

By 1910, roughly 10,000 Greek-owned businesses existed in Chicago. Nearly 130 Greek commercial locations have been identified along the axis of Harrison, Halsted, and Blue Island. The New Era Building, at the very apex of the Delta intersection, was the tallest structure outside of the Loop when it first opened. By 1920 into 1930, the community was flourishing. Residences for the Greek immigrants were built; newspapers, professional services, and fraternal and benevolent associations were created. Peddlers had long abandoned their street vehicles and in rented stores, started shoe-shine shops, flower shops, restaurants and candy stores. Eventually Greek entrepreneurs were so successful they gained control of the retail and wholesale food industry. The Delta flourished.

At the Square Deal Grocery and Meat Market on 71st and Harvard Avenue, circa mid-1920s. Gus Theodoropoulos is holding the telephone, and an unidentified butcher stands behind the counter. John Theodoropoulos, part of the family business, also poses for the photographer.

GREEK BUSINESSES AROUND THE DELTA, CIRCA 1950.

Acropolis Restaurant & Tavern
Arcadia Bakery
Athenian Candle Mfg. Co.
Athenian Candy
Athens Grocery Store
Athens Restaurant
Atlas Pharmacy
Crete Coffee House
Collia's Funeral Parlor
Collia's Grocery Store
Damianos Printers
Deligiannis Greek Grocery
Dianna's Greek Store
Doukas Hay and Grain
Elias Coffee House
Elliopoulos Music Store
Eptanison Bakery
Galanopoulos Leather Shop

Gramatikakis Photographer
Greek Art Printing Co.
Greek Village Restaurant
Greek Press (Paul Javaras, Ed.)
Halls for Greek Brotherhood
    Societies, Brotherhood of
    Messinia, Sparta, Arcadia, etc.
Halsted Jewelry Store
Hellas Greek Restaurant
International Greek Restaurant
John Psihalinos Undertaker
Kalamata Coffee House
Kalavreta Coffee House
Kastritis Travel Agency
Kentrikon Coffee House
Kentrikron Music Store
Kephalonia Coffee House
Kesaris and Rikos Grocery

Kournelis Bakery
Kynouria Coffee House
"L" Restaurant
Makedonia Greek Restaurant
Mallars Wholesale Greek
    Grocery Store
Mandakas Jewelry Store
Mavritsas Coffee House
Melissa Candle
Messinia Grocery Store
Minerva Gambling House
Muzakiotis Music Store
New Agora Meat Market
New Congress Hotel
Parthenon Restaurant
Phoenix Pastry Shop
Pilafas Greek Grocery Store
Poulakos Bakery

Psihalinos Wholesale Butcher
Sarantakis Greek Grocery Store
Seven Seas Restaurant (upstairs
    headquarters for Hellenic
    Brotherhood of Messenia
    and Macedonian Society-
    Alexander the Great)
Shoe Repair and Shoe Shine
Soter's Shoe Shine Supplies
Sparta Coffee House
Stamos Store Fixtures
Sterea Ellas Coffee House
Syros Greek Pastry Shop
Thessalia Greek Restaurant
Trianon Pharmacy
Verros Travel Agency
Villa Theater
White Star Barber Shop

James Lalagos, at left above, began his own import business in 1940, importing Feta cheese in barrels, and olives from Greece. The shipments arrived and were repacked in his own special brine. He imported so much his children could tell by the smell if a shipment was good or not. He arrived in Chicago in 1918 as "Demetrios" but changed his name to "James," making the statement that America was to be his new home. When these photos were taken he was known from coast to coast as the main connection to the delicacies of the Greek homeland. Photo above right shows the interior of his grocery store.

Ted Pilafas owned Washington Dairy Company and was the first to supply Greek yogurt. A truck for business became a moving billboard for the company. Looking at each of these photos, one can see how the number of digits changed in the phone number system over the years.

"My grandfather began 'Harris Motor Express' in the 1920s with little more than a horse and wagon to deliver produce from the wholesale produce markets to mom-and-pop grocery stores. By the third generation, the company owned a number of trucks that would haul produce from boxcars to the markets and make deliveries for the wholesale distributors."

"We had a couple of trucks and we used to distribute foods to restaurants, institutions, and stores. We used to go to South Water Market and buy the stuff and deliver it out to them."

From 1927 to 1966, Plaza Cleaners and Dyers served as a wholesale drycleaner operated by Arthur H. Peponis, and his son, Harold A. Peponis. The custom-designed trucks included side bars on the windows to help prevent theft.

Anthony Mallers picks up produce from the South Water Street Market to deliver to wholesale customers.

Stavros Stratigakis, at right in photo, came to America from Greece in 1922 at the age of 17 with $3.00 in his pocket. At Ellis Island he changed his name to the more English-sounding Steven Stratton. He had heard of the opportunities in America and thought the streets were paved with gold. Steve was lucky enough to have an uncle in the cleaning business in Quincy, Illinois, and went to work for him in 1923. Steve pressed men's clothes and learned how to renovate men's hats. In 1925, Steve came to Chicago and with $50 started his own little hat renovation and shoe shine shop.

After living in Chicago for a few years he met and married Sophia Chibukas. They had their first son, George, in 1929, later followed by William, Leon, Elaine, and James. The business survived the Depression of the 1930s and prospered during the 1940s. Steve was now renovating hats for most all of the major department stores. By 1972, the retailing, renovating, and manufacture of men's dress hats took a total backseat to the manufacture of uniform hats. George became president of the company.

Although Steve was now semi-retired, he was still working as "you could not get that eastern European work ethnic out of him." The company started making hats for the U.S. military in the mid-1970s and continues to this day. Steve's grandson, Steven G. Stratton II, is now the president of Stratton Hats.

Steve turned 100 years old in February 2005, and has received a plaque from President George Bush.

Shown here is a typical counter restaurant in the Greektown neighborhood. This one is owned by Tony, Chris, and John Tomaras (center three men) and was located across from Hull House. At far left is Venette Askounes Ashford (nee Tomaras) who worked in her brothers' restaurant and became protegé to the esteemed Jane Addams, working for the Immigrant Protective League. She not only aided in the immigration of more than 5,000 Greeks, she also helped them to find jobs to begin their new lives and careers in the United States.

Louis, Gus, and Stanley Malleris at their Corner Fountain located at 51st and Western in the 1940s.

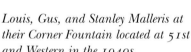

"In the '20s, there was a large influx of immigrants who did not have families to cook for them. There was the single man, away from home, who had to eat out. He flocked to the little neighborhood grill. That expanded into a coffee shop. Greeks progressed from being patrons to being the dominant force in the coffee shop industry. It started with the Greeks who came in the '20s, '30s and '40s. The only job that they could get was in the restaurants. Most Greek immigrants were laborers— carpenters, electricians, factory workers— who found that the restaurant business rewarded their hard work and long hours with far greater benefits than any other profession."
— *Jim Contis*

Alexandra Dalianis, left, and Irene Dalianis work at their husbands' grill at Armitage and Grand around 1941. Aristides and Tom Dalianis came to Chicago at the beginning of the 20th century. They progressed from day laborers to vegetable peddlers to owners of an ice cream parlor, and finally became involved in real estate, also opening the grill pictured below. In 1928, they returned to Greece to marry and brought their families to Chicago prior to the start of World War II.

The last booth in the grill also served as an area for their children to complete their homework after school. As they grew, the youngsters helped out at the grill. Aristides and Tom retired at the ages of 82 and 80, respectively, and enjoyed their years of retirement with their families.

One of the first Greek families to enter the candy business was the Spiro family, who came to America from Kosmas, Arcadia, about the time of the 1893 Columbian Exhibition. Their first store was located at 55th and Cottage Grove and sold handmade candy and hand-dipped chocolates.

George Terevolos stands amongst rows of neatly arranged fruit at his Palace Food Mart on West Chicago Avenue, circa 1920s-'30s.

Peter Panagiotaris branched off from his father's greengrocer business, Stanley's Fresh Fruit, to open a contemporary fine food and fruit market in Chicago's West Loop area where the Randolph Street fruit and vegetable market originally operated.

SWEET GREEKS

From hand-dipped chocolate confections to the creamiest of ice creams, Greeks have all the makings of success in the candy business–a solid work ethic and familiarity with kitchens and restaurants. It has even been reported that the first soda fountain was in a Greektown restaurant.

Greeks entered the industry in the late 1800s with the first wave of Greek migration to Chicago. Ingredients were cheap and sweets were in demand. One of the first to enter this arena was the Spiro family in 1893. According to Demetri Spiro, son of founder Michael Spiro, "The Greeks brought their candy cookbooks and recipes with them."

For some, getting into the confectionery business was the only way to survive during Prohibition, when candy was the only legal vice in town. Even during the Depression, when there was little to do, candy stores provided a wholesome escape for the entire family.

Others started their confectionery business selling fresh fruit or tobacco. But when Cracker Jack popcorn and candy bars were introduced around World War I, many began making their own candies. And in the 1920s, when movie theaters were opening, these entrepreneurs identified the opportunity to sell ice cream and candy to theater-goers and started stores next to theaters.

More often than not, second- and third-generation family members took over the business from their founding father. As young children they remember being introduced to the business at an early age–seating customers, dipping chocolate, or riding the trucks.

Quality is the most important ingredient in the business. And the sweet smell of success was a special treat for companies such as Chicago Candy, Cupid Candies, Dove, Andees, Margies', Gayety's and Homer's, as a sampling of Greeks that found a way into America's heart and sweet tooth.

Although most Greek immigrants initially settled in Chicago, some found opportunity in other midwest towns. One such city was Bloomington where the Princess Confectionery, above, was established.

Owner Christ Phillos and staff inside the Princess Confectionery, circa 1900. The first soda fountain actually originated in a Greektown ice cream parlor.

Leo Stefanos, like most successful Greek business owners, came from humble beginnings immigrating in 1935. He settled on Chicago's South Side working as a dishwasher then as an extra pair of hands in his brother's candy store. Fueled by a desire to succeed, Stefanos opened up his own candy store in 1939 nestled next to the Ace Theater on 63rd and Halsted. In 1941, Leo had a new store at 6838 South Halsted and he needed a name. Looking through the newspaper he noticed a photo of a dove holding an olive branch, a symbol of peace—so he named his store Dove. It was here these humble immigrant hands created one of America's most well-known summer staples: the Dove Ice Cream Bar. Because sons Mike, Chris, and daughter, Amy, were lured not by candy-covered shelves but by the ice cream truck, Leo created his own ice cream bar to keep his kids happy. Son Mike notes, "Men like my father succeed because of their drive to provide for their families. I don't know who implanted this gene in that tiny country [Greece] but we all possess the very same thing." Mike's sharp marketing of Dove candies to banquet halls and grocery stores soon moved Dove Ice Cream bars to nationally recognized status. In 1985, he teamed up with M&M/Mars, also a family company, becoming president of the ice cream division.

"So, there is quite a history of the candy business in Chicago. What is interesting is that early on, every major crossing in Chicago, all the way down Halsted, Ashland, Western, State Street, you name it, almost every corner had an ice cream store."

The original Homer's ice cream store in Wilmette. Steve and Dean Poulos of family-owned Homer's, still operate two stores and also distribute hand-made ice cream to over 400 businesses and distributors around the country.

Leo Stefanos oversees employees at Dove Candies on 6838 South Halsted in the 1940s.

Jim Papageorge, founder of Gayety candies, tends to the register. Gayety's opened its doors in 1920 next door to a movie theater at 91st and Commercial. During that era, ice cream and candy to theater-goers went hand in hand for a special night out. Gayety's is one of the oldest family-owned ice cream parlors in Chicago.

George and Margie Poulos stand at the soda fountain at Margie's on Western Avenue which has been serving homemade ice cream, candy, and fudge sauce for over 88 years. Recipes were shared in the basement by the grandfather, and taught to Margie's proprietors and other relatives owning sweet shops—thus creating a lifetime of family memories of working in the family business.

"My father and I never went anywhere socially together. We never went to a ball game or anything like that. We were very close because we were in the business all of the time, so I spent a lot of time with him and so I got to know his mind."

Father and son, Lee and Jim Flessor, carry on the tradition of Gayety candies which has been satisfying customer's sweet cravings for over 85 years.

Son Peter Poulos serves up homemade ice cream at Margie's Candy and Ice Cream Shop.

John Melonides in 1950 works at the first chair in his shop at 1043 Wilson Avenue.

Bill and Mary Kakavas celebrate the grand opening of Thirteen Colonies Banquet Hall in River Grove in 1967. The hall was host to many church and school fund-raising events for 39 years, until this philanthropic husband and wife team sold the facility in 1996.

"We did not have a lot of money, and yet we were never in need. My dad, being a barber, was always taking in something, whether it was 10 or 24 cents a haircut. There was always something there. We always had a meal on the table."

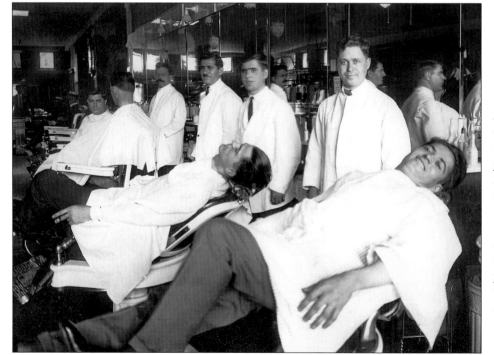

After fleeing Turkey in 1914 to avoid conscription into the Turkish military, and following several years in South America, John Melonides, second from right, arrived in Chicago in the early 1920s. He had learned his trade in Turkey and found employment at a shop, pictured at left, near Wilson and Broadway. A few years later he purchased his own barber shop. He retired from his profession in 1980 at the age of 86.

GreekStar *editor, Nicholas Phillipedes, who served the paper from 1953 to 1994.*

Greek Star *editor, Diane Adam, and Frank Kamberos, chairman, continue to bring the Greek community weekly news and events over a century after the paper's founding by Peter S. Lambros in 1904.*

To keep Greeks in America informed of the news in their homeland, a variety of newspapers were published in Chicago. Soon however, events in the United States took center stage as well as reporting on developments in the Greek American community in Chicago. Some publications lasted less than a year, some many years. The Greek Star, which was originally printed in Greek, below, but after a few years incorporated the English language, has been serving Greek Americans for over 100 years.

Since 2001, the newest publication serving the Greek community is GreekCircle *magazine led by Christopher Ganos, business development director; Alexa Ganakos, publisher; and Connie Kakavas Lissner, editor.*

Efthemia and Themistocles Godelas, original owners of Athenian Candle Company, stand in front of their Halsted Street store. Now, Jean and Thomas Paspalas (second generation), along with their three children, Helen, A. Thomas, and Themis (third generation) keep the family tradition alive as proprietors of the Athenian Candle Company which still prospers on Halsted Street today. Athenian Candle manufactures and sells thousands of hand-dipped beeswax and paraffin candles each year to churches of all denominations nationwide. Also, in the celebration of other sacraments and ceremonies of Greek American life, the company supplies religious icons, stefana *(wedding crowns), baptismal ribbons, gold crosses, oil lamps, cemetery lamps, incense, and censors.*

The grandson of Themistocles Godelas, Themis Paspalas, demonstrates the family's art of candle making.

Three generations ago, owner Themistocles Godelas poses inside the original Athenian Candle store in the 1940s at 747 South Halsted Street across from Hull House. After the city zoned the old Greektown neighborhood for urban redevelopment, he moved the store north of this original site in 1961 to its present location at 300 South Halsted Street.

Early churches used rounded candle stands and were placed near a structure holding a holy icon for the faithful to venerate.

Selling various-sized candles at the Central Candle store on Blue Island Avenue.

THE CHURCH

The Greek Orthodox Church was the instrument that formed and coalesced the Greek community in Chicago. Not only did the newly arrived families find spiritual strength and a place to celebrate and worship, but also the church became the focal point of social and family life and a place where mutual interest organizations formed. Furthermore, promoting knowledge of Greek language, culture, and the Orthodox faith was a high immigrant priority. Thus, within the confines of the church organization, these goals could be readily met.

Beyond instilling in children the faith of their ancestors, the church also was a leveler–articulating common-held beliefs that created strong bonds which overcame normal social and economic barriers. Informal socializing centered around promoting the arts in music, dance, and theatre. Moreover, when there was strife or war in the homeland, the church provided relief efforts along with a host of ongoing charitable activity.

As the largest of numerous Orthodox jurisdictions in the Chicago region, the history of the Metropolis of Chicago dates back to 1923 and was designated the Second Diocese District of North and South America.

Architecturally, the earlier structures were often acquired from other faith groups but within recent decades Metropolis churches have integrated traditional Byzantine forms. The Chicago Metropolis consists of 34 parishes with an additional 26 in the Midwest and embraces approximately a quarter million people.

Color images of churches in this section are from *Ecclesia,* a publication by Panos Fiorentinos.

Organized in 1892, Annunciation was the first Greek Orthodox community in Chicago. Immigrants from Sparta and Laconia successfully petitioned the Synod of Bishops of the Church of Greece to send a priest.

The present Annunciation church was built in 1914 on LaSalle Street. The edifice was modeled after the Athens Cathedral and remains the oldest surviving building in Chicago constructed as a Byzantine church. As parishioners moved north the parish council organized St. Demetrios Church and parochial school, on the northwest side of the city. The church interior was painted in the Byzantine style. The Cathedral continues to be a center of ministry to the Metropolis as well as a center for the Orthodox faith in downtown Chicago.

Holy Trinity, founded in 1897, organized the first continuous Greek Orthodox house of worship in Chicago. The original building, at left, was located on Peoria Street on the near West Side. The first Divine Liturgy was celebrated on October 18, 1897 with 700 in attendance. Meeting the needs of its members, Socrates School, the first Greek Orthodox day school outside Greece, opened in 1908.

St. George Greek Orthodox Church was established in Chicago's Lincoln Park neighborhood in 1923. Founding families were originally members of Annunciation but split over political issues of the day in their homeland. The new congregation purchased a German-Lutheran church, built in 1886, renovating it for Orthodox worship.

A new era began for Holy Trinity in 1963, when the original church was demolished to make way for the University of Illinois at Chicago (UIC) campus. In 1967, the current home was established at 6041 West Diversey Avenue, photo above, where the community celebrated many of its Centennial events in 1997. Another milestone was 1976 when the new school facility as well as the St. Dionysius Chapel opened.

Structurally solid, the 120-year-old stately edifice added an educational wing and in the 1990s a large community center. Located in the affluent Lincoln Park neighborhood, the St. George congregation has grown as it meets local needs.

St. Nicholas was the first church to serve the growing South Side suburbs at 60th and Peoria in the 1920s.

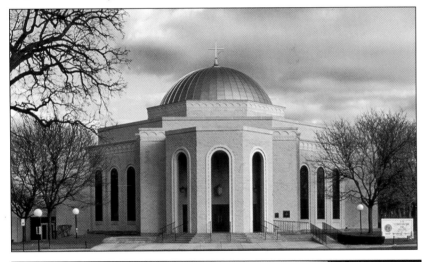

Saint Demetrios of Chicago, originally part of the Annunciation Parish, was organized to serve the Greek population on the northwest side. Services and Solon Greek School began in the "new" building in 1928, just before the Depression. As the area recovered, the Greek population in the neighborhood grew and so did St. Demetrios. In the 1960s the community consisted of 1800 families. In 1963, St. Demetrios underwent considerable expansion to its facilities. A gymnasium, library, cultural center, and new classrooms were added. Since then, the church has seen other significant renovations.

Founded in 1909, Sts. Constantine & Helen has erected four churches in three locations. Originating as a branch of Holy Trinity to serve Chicago's South Side, members established a 1910 church at 61st and Michigan. This structure was destroyed by fire in 1926. A decision was made to rebuild a basilica-style facility on the same site. During the Depression the church fell on hard times. Even after recovering the congregation felt it was time to relocate. The third church was established in the affluent South Shore area in the late 1940s. This magnificent building was one of the largest Greek Orthodox churches in the United States. Reluctantly relocation again became imminent, and in 1976, the community erected its current school and church, at left center, in Palos Hills. An impressive gold dome highlights the complex. The interior dome, at left, captures the transition from the earthly to heavenly by a graduation from dark orange to a brilliant yellow.

At left: Founded in 1925, Assumption Church was formed to serve what was once the far West Side of Chicago. Proximity to the end of a streetcar line accounted for part of the church's rapid early growth. The original facility was made of wood and had sheets hung on ropes to divide the worship space into classrooms. In 1937 on the same site, members erected the current building, designed in traditional Byzantine style. By 1953, Assumption was recognized as the largest Greek Orthodox church in Chicago. During the 1950s the fellowship hall was converted into St. Catherine's Chapel to accommodate the church's religious education program. During this era, Sunday School attendance reached 2,000 children.

The art and architecture of Assumption Church, at right, are identified in four styles: Renaissance, Neo-Byzantine, Classical, and Byzantine. The Renaissance icon of the Pantocrator returns the worshiper to the era in which the building was erected.

For their 75th anniversary members raised funds to renovate and also to restore icons on the walls, ceiling, and the dome. The major renovation was led by interior designer John Regas, whose parents helped to build the church. Assumption continues as a vital center of ministry, where many an assistant priest has begun their service.

St. Basil claims the distinction of originating in a synagogue. Built in 1911, the structure, at left, with classic Greek facade was consecrated in 1927 as the Church of St. Basil. The current altar, with Father Chris Kerhulas presiding, at right, unites past and present reflecting the unique history of this congregation and worship space.

In the early years, many Greek Orthodox churches carried the beautifully decorated Kouvouklion *(funeral bier), containing the* Epitaphios *(embroidered icon of Christ in the tomb) along the streets of Chicago and faithful parishioners and on-lookers alike participated in funeral marches on Good Friday of Holy Week. The photo below shows the Holy Trinity Church procession coming down Blue Island Avenue on Good Friday, circa 1940. Later, congregants from St. Basil would also proceed from their church in the area, and the congregations would meet up together at the corner of Harrison, Halsted, and Blue Island carrying the* Epitaphios *and mourning Christ's death in the Greektown Delta neighborhood.*

Today, on Holy Friday thousands of parishioners still walk in the candlelit procession.

St. Demetrios Greek Orthodox Church of Chicago is filled with candles to celebrate the resurrection of Christ.

"On the evening of April 14, Halsted Street was filled with worshippers in the Greek Good Friday procession. According to custom, the line of march was halted in front of Hull House and a prayer in appreciation of Miss Addams was repeated."

—Prayer in front of Hull House
Hull House, Quarterly Report,
July 1, 1944

The Agiasmos *(blessing of the building site of a church) is performed at Sts. Constantine & Helen Greek Orthodox Church at its second location at 74th and Stoney Island. In 1948, the congregation broke ground and built the basement to hold services, then they proceeded to construct the main floor, which is pictured being blessed by holy water.*

"There wasn't a parish in the area, so a bunch of people got together and they decided to start a church. We first started off in a gymnasium of a school called Nixon school. And, from there we bought a little church. And, then we built this church."

—Holy Apostles Greek Orthodox Church in Westchester, Illinois

Archbishop Iakovos peforms the ceremony of "Opening of the Doors" at St. Nicholas Greek Orthodox Church in Oak Lawn, Illinois, at their second location in 1974. His Eminence knocks three times on the doors of the church with a staff.

The consecration (opening dedication) of St. John the Baptist Greek Orthodox Church in Des Plaines, Illinois, is performed by His Eminence Metropolitan Iakovos in 1971. During the consecration services, the Holy Relics are placed in the church entombed in the altar.

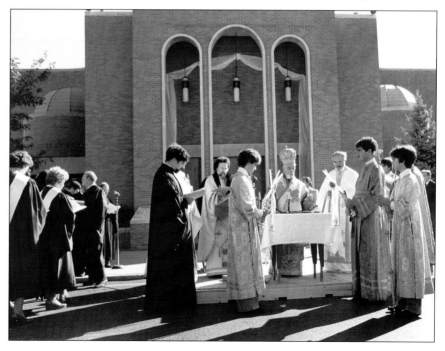

The fundraising committee of Sts. Constantine & Helen Greek Orthodox Church, located at 7351 South Stoney Island, gather for a meeting and a group photo in 1946. Sts. Constantine & Helen moved to their current location in Palos Hills in 1976.

The Philoptochos of Annunciation Cathedral serves the congregation led by Reverend Father Kesses, circa 1940. The Philoptochos is the philanthropic arm of the church and the word means "friend of the poor." Its goals and purposes are "Philanthropy, Propagation of Faith, and Education and Training." Philoptochos was first established in the United States in 1931 and it is the largest Christian women's philanthropic organization in the country.

The 1989-91 Chicago Diocesan Philoptochos Board.

Members of the Philoptochos of St. Basil Greek Orthodox Church faithfully serve the hungry using the Annunciation Cathedral facilities. Each chapter that hosts the luncheon is responsible for the menu, cooking, serving, and cleanup.

Twice a month, 22 Philoptochos chapters in Chicago rotate the responsibilities of feeding about 150 people through the "Feed the Hungry" program at the Annunciation Bessie Miller Cathedral Hall.

The Ladies Philoptochos, in partnership with the Bishop's Task Force on AIDS, created a metropolis-wide annual Lenten "Quiltathon" to make handmade quilts specifically for the infants and children with HIV/AIDS. The bright and soft quilts help give comfort to children's extended stays in the hospital. The items were delivered by the Very Reverend Archimandrite Demetri Kantzavelos and representatives of Philoptochos to Children's Memorial Hospital. Since the "Quiltathon" began in 1999, over 2,000 quilts have been made and distributed to hospitals in the U.S. and the Ukraine.

LEADERSHIP

If a person has a natural gift of leadership and an ability to inspire devotion or enthusiasm in others, he is said to have "charisma," which in Greek translates into "gift." There are many gifted leaders of our Greek American community, many more than appear on these pages or even in this book.

Over the years, they have led the many Greek organizations and committees by example, so others are motivated to follow. They have built buildings and churches, have impacted government policies, and helped those in need. It is our hope that future generations of Greek Americans will be inspired by the dedication of our community leaders, beginning with the early immigrants, as they have all contributed to make a name for Greek Americans all over the world.

Maria Pappas faithfully serves Chicago as Cook County Treasurer.

"With regard to excellence, it is not enough to know, but we must try to have and use it." –Aristotle

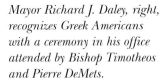

Mayor Richard J. Daley, right, recognizes Greek Americans with a ceremony in his office attended by Bishop Timotheos and Pierre DeMets.

George Stephanopoulos, Michael Dukakis, and Andrew Athens, president of the Council for Hellenes Abroad, enjoy a moment together.

NBC Newscaster, Anna Davlantes, introduces honored Greek Americans. Pictured, left to right, are Betty Gritzanis; George Loukas, Cubby Bear Restaurants; Anthony Nichols, Central Savings Bank; Dr. Dochios Kamberos, Hellenic Museum and Greek Nursing Home benefactor; The Very Reverend Archimandrite Demetri Kantzavelos; Elaine Drikakis, executive director of the Hellenic Museum; Christopher Janus, author; and Tom Diamond, president of the Greek American Restaurant Association.

In 2002, Consul General Gabriel Kopsides and His Eminence Metropolitan Iakovos arrive at a function.

"I like the commitment that we share. An intense feeling of responsibility as citizens: That we feel strongly that we should be well informed. That we should participate. That we should be civically engaged. That if we want a good government, we have to work very hard to get it, and step forward. And we believe in very strong leadership."

The first Greek American to hold an executive office in Cook County, Nicholas J. Melas, stands near the Nicholas J. Melas Centennial Fountain dedicated to him for his over 30 years of service to the Metropolitan Water Reclamation District of Greater Chicago.

Paul Vallas, CEO of the School District of Philadelphia and former CEO of the Chicago Public Schools, is honored for his leadership in education by the United Hellenic American Congress. Pictured, from left to right, are Michael Skoubis, Paul Vallas, James Regas, John Marks (current Hellenic Museum board president), and Geri Chico.

Senator Adeline J. Geo-Karis, seated, is joined by the Mayor of Athens Greece, Dora Bakoyannis, left, and GreekCircle Publisher, Alexa Ganakos, when the Mayor visited Chicago in honor of the 2004 Athens Olympic Games. Senator Geo-Karis is Assistant Majority Leader of the State Senate and has served in the Illinois State Legislature since 1972. She was the second Greek woman to become a lawyer in the State of Illinois. Moreover, she was recognized as one of the first female lawyers in the Navy's Judge Advocate Corps and rose to the rank of lieutenant commander.

Pictured, left to right, at a Hellenic Museum fundraising event are Chris Tomaras, vice president of SAE/North and South America; Janet Carlson, museum board member; Andrew Athens, president of the World Council of Hellenes Abroad and national chairman of the United Hellenic American Congress; James M. Mezilson, a museum founder; and Dino Amiraros, past museum board president.

"I want to make a difference. I think that everybody really wants to have a life with meaning and that makes a difference. That's part of my Greek values. I mean, you have to make the world a better place, that's what I was taught."

Governor Whitcomb of Indiana, Mrs. Richard Ogilvie (wife of Illinois Governor Ogilvie), Stacy Diacou, Vice President Spiro Agnew, and Nicholas Manos enjoy a seat at the head table during a Greek formal function at the Congress Hotel in 1970.

Past presidents of the Stereapaton Society conduct a meeting: left to right, Christ Petros, Tom Tom Bakery; Rev. Daniel Gambrilis, St. Nicholas Church; Louis Contos; Gust Pappas, Pappas Construction; and Takis Christopoulos.

Angelo G. Geocaris, attorney; James M. Mezilson, a founding member of the Hellenic Museum; Harry Mark Petrakis, author; and Andrew T. Kopan, educator and historian gather in Greektown to celebrate Mezilson's 80th birthday and 60 years of writing for the Greek Press newspaper.

Representatives of the Greek Food Industry sign donation checks for the Hellenic Museum. Seated are Jim Contis, publisher of Food Industry News and Sam Stavrakas, Cosmopolitan Textile. Standing are Stan Greanias, Superior Coffee; unidentified, and Peter Parthenis, Grecian Delight.

The fellowship group, the Levendes ("The Strong and the Proud"), brings together doctors, lawyers, educators, businessmen, real estate developers, and clergy once a month to keep alive strong bonds to their Greek ancestry. This group, co-founded by George Skontos and Peter J. Cappas, is made up of first-generation Greeks. Many share friendships that started in Koraes School, Sts. Constantine & Helen Church, Morgan Park Military Academy, and the University of Illinois at Navy Pier.

Founded in 1993 by Elias Voulgaris, the Hellenic Police Association was created to foster and promote unity among law enforcement officers of Hellenic heritage. Besides promoting Greek culture, they also provide law enforcement and safety awareness to the citizens of the Hellenic community. Members work on the local, state, and federal level, and include various law enforcement agencies including the State's Attorney's office.

Members of the Hellenic Professional Society of Illinois gather at a banquet at the Bismark Hotel in 1958. HPSI was founded in 1925: to encourage and promote education and learning; to cooperate with other organizations promoting the arts, letters, and sciences; to uphold the dignity of the professions represented by its members; and to cultivate fellowship opportunities.

Ted Spyropoulos, President of ENOSIS, with honorary president of Plant Your Roots in Greece, Senator Hillary Clinton. The Foundation, through donor contributions, brings back the greenery to Greece by reforesting. The first forest was planted in 1999 in Sounion which was devastated by forest fires.

RESTAURANT RECIPES

The often-repeated phrase "Let's meet in Greektown," is warmly said by Chicagoans when suggesting where to share a meal together. Greektown, amazingly, with its familiar surroundings, keeps drawing generations of locals. Despite its relative size, Greektown possesses some of the finest Greek restaurants in the country. Four of the best are Costa's, Greek Islands, Parthenon, and Pegasus who have contributed some of their more popular recipes. A majority of the following dishes were created by the chefs from each of these award-winning establishments. Even though their past patrons have included nationally known figures and celebrities, guests will not only enjoy a great meal, they will leave feeling they have just visited the warm and friendly country of Greece.

Costa's

"Unique and high quality food offerings is the name of the game," says Christ Demos, owner of Costa's Restaurant. With two locations–Greektown, which opened in 1993 and Oak Brook Terrace in 1996, Costa's indeed serves up unique dishes that take the traditional meal to the next level.

Demos, along with managing partner Nick Nicolaou, pictured left, purchased Costa's in 1999. Demos has been in the restaurant business since 1953. "I came to the U.S. in 1951 to study chemical engineering," he explained. "Times were tough, and school would have taken 14 years to complete. I had to help support the family, so I went to work in the restaurants." He sought help from his uncle, Gus Douvikas, who along with James Lalagos owned the Acropolis Restaurant and Tavern in old Greektown. Lalagos sponsored Chris Demos' passage to the States, and so they were very close. Demos went to work for his uncle, Gus Douvikas and Lalagos. As he states, he learned everything he knows about the restaurant business and Greek cuisine, from those two gentlemen. "Lessons I will never forget."

Demos had established his first restaurant in 1953. He has owned a total of 33 restaurants since then, all over Chicago and the suburbs, and even in Galveston, Texas. "I wanted to come to Greektown," Demos revealed, "to be a more active part of the Greek community and enhance the current offerings for Greek cuisine." He had dined at other restaurants on the street, and though very good in their own right, he felt it was time "to innovate," to incorporate other Mediterranean influences, and at the same time take the traditional dishes, add a few twists and elevate them to a whole new plateau.

Nicolaou was an old friend, and had grown up working in a slew of ethnic restaurants, everything from German to Greek. Demos and Nicolaou, both from near Tripolis, Greece, had a similar philosophy, in terms of what sort of menu they wanted to contribute to Greektown. Thus, a partnership was born. Together with their chef, they have created dishes based on authentic recipes with an added flair, from all over Greece. They import the finest of ingredients, and taste test every recipe before it reaches the menu. If it does not delight their discriminating palates, it isn't good enough for their customers.

Costa's is *Zagat* rated, among the top 10 restaurants in Chicago. Many famous and influential people have dined there, including United States General Richard Mayers, who called it his favorite place in town. ABC Channel 7's food critic James Ward, also frequents Costa's, and consistently gives it high marks.

Demos and Nicolaou are committed to continually evolving their menu, transferring the imagination and creativity of their partnership into delectable and innovative Greek crusine.

GRILLED RACK OF LAMB

A perennial favorite, lamb is served in every Greek home and restaurant.
Costa's version includes time to marinate the meat, which allows the spices
and meat to converge and bring out even more of the succulent flavors.

INGREDIENTS

2 racks of lamb, approximately 2-1/2 lbs.,
*   trimmed of excess fat*
extra virgin olive oil
1 lemon
1 tsp. oregano
1/2 tsp. salt
1/3 tsp. black pepper

Metaxa is a traditional
Greek liqueur. This special
edition bottle is a depic-
tion of the Greek Evzone,
or Royal guard.

Combine spices in a small bowl, and then rub on meat. Brush with oil. Cover and refrigerate meat for one hour.

Preheat broiler or grill, and brush some oil on the pan or rack. When cooking surface is hot, cook lamb for about 15 minutes if you prefer it rare, or 25 minutes for medium. Turn occasionally for thorough cooking.

Serve whole or cut from the bone. Sprinkle with fresh lemon juice and oregano. Vegetables and pasta, rice or oven roasted potatoes, make wonderful accompaniments.

SERVES 2

STUFFED GRILLED KALAMARI

Another item on Costa's menu is a variation on the more common grilled squid. "Kalamari" is the Greek word for squid. We add the wonderful flavors of Feta and Kefalotiri cheeses to create this superlative dish.

INGREDIENTS

12 squids, each approximately 7-8 inches long
1 lb. Feta cheese, cut into small pieces
1 lb. Kefalotiri cheese, cut into small pieces
6 sprigs fresh parsley, finely chopped
6 sprigs fresh dill, finely chopped
pinch of red pepper flakes
pinch of oregano
pinch of black pepper
1/2 cup extra virgin olive oil

VINAIGRETTE DRESSING:

1/2 cup extra virgin olive oil
1/4 cup balsamic vinegar
1/4 tsp. oregano
salt, to taste

Under running water, clean the squid, making sure to not cut the sac. In a large bowl, combine the cheeses, oil, and spices. Stuff the squid with the cheese mixture and then brush with olive oil.

Preheat broiler or grill and oil the rack. Transfer squid to the grill, and turn occasionally for about 10 minutes, or until browned. Dress with the vinaigrette. To serve as an appetizer, cut into bite-sized pieces.

SERVES 6 AS MAIN COURSE; 12 AS APPETIZER

BAKLAVA

A traditional dessert served throughout the Mediterranean, it is a great way to cap off a delicious meal. For an extra special flavor, we have added cloves to our version.

INGREDIENTS

1 cup (8 oz.) melted unsalted butter
1 lb. blanched almonds, finely chopped
1/4 cup sugar
2 tsp. cinnamon
1/4 tsp. ground cloves
1 lb. phyllo pastry sheets

SYRUP:

7 oz. sugar
12 oz. honey
2 cups water
juice of 1 lemon
2 whole cloves
sliver of lemon rind

Preheat oven to 350 degrees. Follow package instructions to thaw phyllo. Brush a 13 x 9 x 2-inch baking pan with melted butter. Place aside.

In a large bowl, combine nuts, sugar, cinnamon, and cloves. Mix well. Place 10 sheets of phyllo dough, one at a time, in the pan, and brush the top of each with butter. Be sure to keep remaining phyllo covered, so it does not dry out. Spoon on some of nut mixture. Add another sheet of phyllo and brush with butter. Repeat. Add some more of the nut mixture. Add two more sheets of phyllo, brushing each with butter. Repeat until you have used all of the nut mixture. Then place 10 sheets of phyllo on top, brushing each sheet with butter. Turn the edges of the phyllo into the pan, and brush the top with the remaining butter. Score the top layer of phyllo with parallel lines. Bake for 1 hour.

To prepare the syrup, combine all ingredients, heat in a saucepan and stir continuously to dissolve sugar. Strain and let cool. Pour half of the syrup over the hot baklava. Let stand for 30 minutes, and then pour on the remainder of the syrup.

YIELDS 30 PIECES

A sampling of the decadent desserts at Costa's. From the traditional galaktobouriko and baklava, to crème caramel and other delights, one cannot pass up dessert!

GRILLED SWORDFISH KEBOB

Seafood is a staple in the Greek culture, and we always seek new and inventive ways to prepare it. Swordfish, called "xifias" in Greek, is a popular fish that can be served in any number of ways. Here's a great recipe that you can recreate at home, in the broiler or even on the backyard grill.

INGREDIENTS
2 lbs. swordfish, cut into
    1-1/2-inch cubes
1 green pepper
1 red pepper
1 medium white onion

MARINADE:
1 cup extra virgin olive oil
juice of 1 lemon
2 garlic cloves, chopped
3 sprigs fresh parsley,
    finely chopped
salt, to taste
pepper, to taste
1/2 tsp. oregano

Prepare the marinade by mixing together all ingredients, well. Chop peppers and onion in large square-sized pieces. Place them in a bowl. Add the swordfish. Sprinkle with 1/4 of the marinade.

Thread fish, peppers, and onions, alternating fish and vegetables, onto 4 long, metal skewers. Pour the remaining marinade over the skewers. Cook in the broiler or on the grill, for about 12 minutes, or until cooked. Turn them so they cook on all sides. Serve with rice pilaf.

SERVES 4

GRILLED OCTOPUS

Octopus is a regular part of any Greek menu. Octopus, comes from the Greek "oktapodi," meaning eight legs. A top seller at Costa's, this dish will get raves at your home, as well.

INGREDIENTS
6 – 1 lb. baby octopus (if frozen thaw, and if fresh, rinse well)
1/2 cup red wine vinegar
1 tsp. whole allspice

VINAIGRETTE:
1 cup extra virgin olive oil
1/4 cup red wine vinegar
1 tsp. dried oregano
pinch of salt

In a 6 or 8 qt. pot, place octopus, vinegar and allspice. Add enough water to cover the octopus. Cook for approximately 20-30 minutes. Place octopus in a colander, to dry and cool. After cooling, cut and discard tentacles. Transfer remaining octopus to a bowl and sprinkle with a pinch of oregano.

Heat broiler or grill to cook, and oil the surface. Place octopus on an oiled rack. Turn occasionally for thorough cooking, about 6 minutes, until browned. Toss with the oil vinaigrette and serve.

SERVES 6

This may also be served as an appetizer in smaller portions.

Greek Islands

Managing partner, Gus Couchell, on a visit to Monemvassia Winery in Greece sampling wines before importing them to the Greek Islands Restaurants.

"One of the oldest spots in Greektown, the Islands is the Premiere spot to dine with a group of friends," wrote *New City* magazine in 2003. This landmark restaurant is among the longest-running, and it has endured for one simple reason–consistently delicious food.

The Greek Islands opened its doors in Greektown in 1971. Gus Couchell, who had worked at some of Chicago's most famous restaurants, met Filandros Sguros, Apostolos Bournas, and Michael Scafidi at the old Athens Restaurant, then located on Rush Street. They agreed to bring their considerable talents together to establish a fine dining restaurant with good food, good service, and a beautiful Greek-inspired setting. "All of us worked together in the restaurant," Couchell recalled, "as cook, waiter, host, bartender, dishwasher, and even going to the local market every morning for fresh supplies." On their first day of business they made $203.

Today they are America's busiest Greek restaurant. With another location in Lombard, the restaurants serve over half a million customers each year. Always one of the highest-rated restaurants in the city, Greek Islands offers the finest cuisine, and continues to flourish as Greektown grows.

The restaurant has received a myriad of accolades, including: Best Ethnic Restaurant – April 2005, *Playboy Magazine*; 3-stars (the only 3-star rating for a Greek restaurant in

Chicago) by the *Chicago Sun-Times* newspaper, and most recently the only Greek restaurant selected for the *Budget Dining Guide* in the November 2005 issue of *Chicago* magazine. Recognized by its peers, Greek Islands was voted into the *Food Industry News* Hall of Fame for Best Greek, Best ethnic dining, as well as Best gyros.

Part of the winning formula is the partners' openness to new ideas. Gus Couchell travels to Greece every year and selects the finest wines and ingredients and ships them directly to the restaurants.

The décor is designed to reflect the Islands, and evokes a feeling that you are actually enjoying the seaside experience. The traditional Greek cuisine is so authentic, like someone's Yiayia (grandmother) spent hours in the kitchen. No passport is required for Greek Islands guests.

The Greek Islands has served as a Greektown landmark for years and, no doubt, for many years to come.

SPANAKORIZO

This vegetarian dish is delicious either warm or cold and can be enjoyed as an entree or a side dish. Mix in a little Feta cheese and some fresh lemon juice to give it a great twist. A traditional dish called spanakorizo, literally meaning spinach and rice, brings together lemon and fresh herbs for a vegetarian delight. Stuffed grape vine leaves, top left, called dolmades, is a favorite Greek dish served with egg lemon sauce. Avgolemono, egg lemon soup, top right, is a wonderful beginning to any Greek meal.

INGREDIENTS

1 lb. fresh chopped spinach
1/2 cup rice
1/2 cup chopped Spanish onions
1/2 cup chopped green onions
1/2 cup extra virgin olive oil
1/2 cup chopped tomato
2 tbsp. tomato paste
1/2 cup dill, chopped
2 cups water
salt and pepper to taste

Sauté the chopped Spanish and green onions in olive oil until lightly brown. Add tomato paste, chopped tomatoes, salt and pepper, then stir for 1 minute. Add spinach and cook for 5 minutes.

Add water and bring to a boil. Mix in rice and cook for 15-20 minutes. Stir in dill a few minutes before finishing.

SERVES 4

ARNI FOURNOU (ROASTED LAMB)

The most popular meat in Greece, lamb, is often served for religious holidays, or special occasions when family and friends gather. It is even great as leftovers; simply add more potatoes and serve!

INGREDIENTS

4 small lamb shanks
1/2 tbsp. oregano
1/4 cup extra virgin olive oil
1/2 cup chopped tomatoes
4 garlic cloves, finely chopped
1 lemon
2 cups water
3 large Idaho potatoes, cut into quarters
salt and pepper to taste

In a bowl, mix the oil and other ingredients, except potatoes. Place the lamb in a deep baking pan, and coat each shank with the oil mixture. Cover the pan with foil and bake at 450 degrees, for 45 minutes. Check the pan during baking, to be sure that some liquid is still in the pan, so lamb stays moist. Add additional, if needed.

Remove the foil and add the potatoes. Baste potatoes with the juice. Bake for an additional 75 minutes.

SERVES 4

SHRIMP TOURKOLIMANO

Shrimp Tourkolimano is a dish with origins from the Greeks of Asia Minor. Its name literally means "Turkish harbor," named for the place where Greeks arrived upon their exodus from that region, at the port of Piraeus. The topping is so good we recommend you dip your bread into it and enjoy!

INGREDIENTS

1 lb. shrimp, peeled and de-veined
1/4 cup extra virgin olive oil
1/2 cup Spanish onions, chopped
1/4 cup green onions, chopped
4 garlic cloves, finely chopped
1/2 cup chopped tomatoes
1/4 cup tomato puree
6 oz. crumbled Feta cheese
1 cup water
salt and pepper to taste

Sauté the garlic, green and Spanish onions in olive oil until lightly brown. Add the tomato puree and chopped tomatoes, then continue cooking for 2-3 minutes. Add the water, salt and pepper, and boil for 10 minutes. Preheat oven to broil.

Add the shrimp and boil for 3-4 minutes. Transfer to a small, shallow baking pan and top with the crumbled Feta. Broil for about 10 minutes, or until the Feta begins to melt and brown.

SERVES 4

Saganaki is always a crowd pleaser, evoking cheers of "OPA" from every table in the room.

LAKE SUPERIOR WHITEFISH
GREEK STYLE

Seafood is found in abundance throughout Greece. Greek Islands Restaurant prepares Lake Superior white-fish using simple, fresh ingredients that bring out the flavor of the fish without overwhelming it.

INGREDIENTS
4-8oz. whitefish fillets
1/2 cup extra virgin olive oil
1/4 cup water
2 oz. lemon juice
1/4 tsp. paprika
salt and oregano to taste

In a shallow baking pan, rub the fillets with 1/4 cup oil, salt, oregano and 1 oz. of lemon juice. Sprinkle the fillets with the paprika and broil on high for 15 minutes.

For a healthful and tasty dressing, take the remaining 1/4 cup of olive oil and 1 oz. of lemon juice and stir vigorously. Lightly pour on the fish for flavor.

SERVES 4

Executive Chef George Bournas proudly prepares authentic Greek cuisine for all to enjoy.

AMBROSIA
(SHREDDED PHYLLO AND WALNUT DESSERT)

This recipe is a Greek Islands' original, utilizing the basic ingredients used in many Greek desserts to create this modern delight. "Ambrosia" is the name given to the foods that the ancient Greek gods ate on Mount Olympus.

INGREDIENTS

1 lb. phyllo dough, shredded (if frozen, defrost before use)
1 lb. walnut meats
1/2 cup sugar
1/4 tsp. ground cinnamon
1/2 cup butter

SYRUP

3 cups water
2 cups sugar
1 cup honey
1 peel of lemon
1 peel of orange

Finely chop the walnuts, add sugar and cinnamon and mix. Melt butter. Pull apart the shredded phyllo dough until it is like fluffy threads. In a small baking pan, use half of the phyllo dough to layer the bottom of the pan. Coat the phyllo with 1/4 cup of the melted butter. Spread the walnut mixture evenly over the phyllo, then use the remaining phyllo as a top layer of dough, spread over the mixture. Coat with the remaining butter and bake for 1 hour at 300 degrees.

To make the syrup, mix all ingredients in a sauce pan and boil for 15 minutes, stirring often. While the dessert is still warm, pour the syrup over it, adding as much as needed to your taste. Serve warm or cold with vanilla ice cream and caramel sauce.

SERVES 4

Parthenon

"Naming our restaurant the Parthenon, carries a deep responsibility for excellence, one that we take very seriously," says founding partner Chris Liakouras. He, along with brother Bill, opened their restaurant in 1968, giving it the name of the majestic structure that sits atop the Acropolis, in Athens, Greece. One of the oldest establishments in the Greektown neighborhood, the Parthenon has grown and expanded over the years. Beginning with a small storefront, the facility currently accommodates up to 300. In addition, there is a banquet hall used for many special events.

Legend has it that flaming saganaki was born here. Long a favorite Greek dish, the idea to flame it, did not come from the motherland. This was a new concept, providing an exciting display that continues to delight diners. The Parthenon has been flaming their cheese and shouting a hearty "OPA!" (with customers joining in), since they opened their doors over 37 years ago. Today, you'll find "flaming" saganaki in fine dining Greek restaurants throughout America and even in some places in Greece!

Chef Sotiris Stasinos joined the staff in 1974, and became a partner in 1997. He adds his own flair to traditional dishes, culminating in a memorable dining experience.

Co-owner Bill Liakouras returned to Greece in 1975. Chris continued on with the family business, and later, his daughter,

Yanna, joined him as a manager, and is now a partner. Together, they take a hands-on approach, and the Parthenon is flourishing under their joint leadership. They are there to greet you when you arrive, and they roll up their sleeves and do whatever it takes to create a superb Parthenon experience for every customer.

The restaurant has earned top ratings from newspapers, magazines and TV critics, including "Best gyros," "Best saganaki," and "Best Greek restaurant."

Long a pillar of the Greektown area, the Parthenon continues its tradition of fine Greek cuisine served with a welcoming smile of hospitality.

BRAISED LAMB – GREEK STYLE

A traditional dish, braised lamb is often served on special occasions. The Parthenon serves it with oven-browned potatoes, orzo or rice, and recommends a Greek red wine, such as a 1994 Naoussa Boutari.

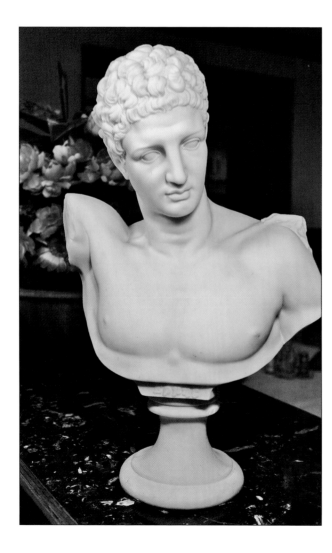

INGREDIENTS

2 *lbs. lamb (shoulder, rib
    or leg, as preferred),
    cut into 2-3-inch pieces*
1 *onion, chopped*
1 *clove garlic, crushed*
1/2 to 3/4 *cup olive oil,
    as needed*
1/2 *cup dry Greek wine
    (Boutari Santorini
    or other)*
2 *bay leaves*
1 *tsp. salt*
1 *tsp. pepper*
1/2 *tsp. nutmeg*
2 *tomatoes, skinned and
    finely chopped*
1/2 *cup tomato paste*
2 *cups water*

Rinse the lamb and pat it dry. Set aside. Place onions and garlic in a large pot, and sauté in olive oil, over medium heat. When onions and garlic begin to sizzle, add lamb and stir, turning lamb pieces for 15 minutes.

Add wine, bay leaves, salt, pepper, nutmeg, and chopped tomatoes. Stir well, then cover the pot. Cook for 15-20 minutes.

In a small bowl, mix the tomato paste and water, and then add to the lamb mixture. Stir, cover the pot again, and cook on a low flame for 2 hours. The lamb is fully cooked when the meat separates easily from the bone.

SERVES 4-6

CHICKEN SOUVLAKI

Chicken Souvlaki (shishkebob) is a lighter, leaner take on the traditional shishkebob. It's one of the most popular dishes at the Parthenon.

INGREDIENTS

2 3-1/2 lb. chickens
1 green pepper
1 tomato
1 onion
1 tbsp. salt
1 tbsp. pepper
1 tbsp. oregano
1 cup vegetable oil
1/2 cup lemon juice
Long shishkebob skewers

Debone the chicken, and then remove the skin. Cut the chicken into cubes. Place in a bowl. Add salt, pepper, oregano, oil, and lemon juice. Mix, using your hands.

Take the green pepper, tomato and onion, and cut each into 4 large pieces. Add these to the mixture. Stir again. Let this stand for one hour.

Place 1 cube of chicken through the skewer, then a piece of green pepper, a piece of chicken, a piece of tomato, a piece of chicken, then a piece of onion, and so on, until you have reached the desired size of the kebob.

Cook in the broiler or on the grill for 15-20 minutes. If the grill is very hot, cooking time may be shorter. Turn occasionally to cook on all sides.

SERVES 4

MELITZANOSALATA

*A delectable spread made from fresh eggplant, melitzanosalata is delicious
served with crusty fresh baked bread.*

INGREDIENTS

5 to 6 eggplants
1 cup olive oil
1/2 cup red wine vinegar
4 oz. parsley, chopped very fine
1/4 head garlic, chopped very fine

Place eggplants in a small dry pan. Do not cut or chop
them. Put in 350 degree oven for 35-40 minutes, to soften.
Turn occasionally. When eggplant skins appear shriveled,
remove from oven. Let cool.

Remove the stem and peel off skin. Cut in half, lengthwise, then remove the inside seeds. Chop the remaining
pulp, then place in a bowl, and add chopped garlic and
parsley. Stir with a wooden spoon, and while stirring, slowly
add oil and vinegar. Continue to stir until oil and vinegar
are mixed in.

Transfer the spread to a clean bowl. Let it cool.
Refrigerate until ready to serve.

SERVES 8

*Everyone shouts "OPA!" What better way to start out a meal than
with the exciting display of a flaming saganaki. The concept of
flaming the saganaki is said to have been created at the Parthenon.*

BROILED RED SNAPPER

Broiled red snapper, a light and delicious seafood dish, is a popular menu item at the Parthenon. This is made with only lemon, olive oil, and oregano, so as not to compete with the fish's delicate flavor. Rice, vegetables or potatoes are tasty options for side-dish accompaniments.

INGREDIENTS
1 whole red snapper (1-2 lbs.)
1 tsp. salt per pound of fish
1/4 cup olive oil
1/4 cup lemon juice
1 tsp. oregano

GARNISH:
Tomato slices
Cucumber slices
Lemon wedges

Scale and clean the fish in very cold water. Pat dry. Make a 1/4-inch deep slit nearly the entire length of each side. Place fish in a broiling pan. Mix salt, oil, lemon juice and oregano. Pour 1/4 of this mixture into another bowl, as you will use that to brush on the fish prior to cooking, and the rest you'll keep to pour over the cooked fish.

Brush the top side of the fish with this mixture. Place the pan in the oven, approximately 10 inches from the flame and broil about 10 minutes. Turn the fish, and brush the other side with the oil mixture. Broil 6 more minutes. Test for doneness. Remove from pan, and place on a platter. Pour the rest of the olive oil mixture over the fish. Garnish with lemon slices, tomato wedges, and cucumber slices.

SERVES 2

VEGETARIAN MOUSSAKA

Moussaka is one of the most challenging Greek dishes to make, but it's worth every tasty morsel. No Greek menu would be complete without this traditional meal.

INGREDIENTS

2 cups vegetable oil

2 medium-sized eggplants

2 potatoes

2 zucchini

1/2 garlic

1/2 lb. margarine

4 oz. parsley

1 1/2 lbs. Kefalotiri cheese, grated

2 cups milk

4 oz. corn starch

Cut the eggplants, potatoes, and zucchini in slices 1/4 -inch thick. Fry these in the vegetable oil along with garlic. Take out of frying pan and let them drain.

In a 12 x 12-inch pan, place the grated Kefalotiri cheese on the bottom. Over the cheese, place a layer of the sliced potatoes, then the zucchini, and then the eggplant. Keep some cheese for later on.

For the Bechamel sauce, boil the milk in a small pot. In another pot, melt the margarine while stirring continuously. Add to this the corn starch and stir. Add the milk and keep stirring. The sauce should be as thick as mashed potatoes. If needed, add some water. Take the pot off the fire. In a bowl beat the eggs, and add them to the pot with the sauce.

Pour Bechamel sauce over the layered vegetables, so that all areas are covered. On top place the remaining Kefalotiri cheese.

Put the pan in a warm oven at 325 degrees for 30 to 45 minutes, till the top of the sauce turns golden brown. Garnish with parsley.

SERVES 4

Pegasus

"At Pegasus, it is like having an open house 365 days of the year. We welcome you as we would to our home," says owner Yiannis Melidis. The simple philosophy, which he shares with partner Tony Katsoulias, of bringing together good food and good people, led to the opening of Pegasus Restaurant in 1990. Then a newcomer to the neighborhood, Pegasus helped to fuel the resurgence of Greektown.

"We wanted to educate our customers about Greece and the wonderful, healthy cuisine," Melidis explained. At that time, people still considered Greek food to be unhealthy. "We had to reeducate the public, and today, the so-called Mediterranean Diet, is prescribed as the healthiest way to eat." Pegasus also became known for slide shows of stunning images from Greece. This, for many non-Greek diners, was their first glimpse of the exotic beauty of the country. The owners felt strongly about sharing every aspect of their homeland–traditional recipes, hospitality, and the landscape. The cuisine is authentic, made from the recipes with which they were raised.

Pegasus is no stranger to the spotlight. Over the years, they have greeted famous guests like musician Yanni, and the restaurant was used by Oprah Winfrey as the setting for the taping of her show promoting the film *My Big Fat Greek Wedding*. Pegasus is also renowned for its amazing roof-top terrace. With exceptional city views, one can dine al fresco and enjoy the accompaniment of live Greek music. The venue is a proven summer favorite for many Chicagoans, both Greek and non-Greek.

With its warm and inviting ambience, Pegasus was

featured in *Bon Appetit* magazine. Equally pleasing to the customer is the Artopolis Café, located just down the street.

Artopolis, which literally means, "town of bread," is one of the newest and most welcome additions to Greektown. "We've combined the elements of bakery, café, bar, gift shop, and coffee house, and it's become a gathering place for young and old," says manager Maria Melidis. This concept is new to Chicago, but very common throughout Greece. Here, one can find artisan breads, traditional Greek sweets, and a full menu, including their signature "Artopita," a dish that combines flaky dough with ingredients such as spinach, Feta, and more, made daily in the open-air kitchen. "The menu items are so unique," adds Maria, "they have been patented." In the café's casual and inviting atmosphere, one can sit back, catch up on some reading, and enjoy a meal, a specialty coffee, or a sumptuous sweet.

Artopolis Bakery and Café continues to evolve above and beyond the traditional image of Greek food. Pegasus Restaurant represents the new age of Greek cuisine and excellence in casual dining.

CHICKEN ALEXANDER
"YEMISTO KOTOPOULO ME SPANAKI"

This creation certainly underscores Pegasus' culinary imprint on Greektown. It is a perfect synthesis of ingredients, wrapped in a spiced-chicken breast fillet.

INGREDIENTS
MARINADE:
1/2 cup olive oil
1/2 cup white wine
2 tbsp. salt
1 tbsp. pepper
1 garlic clove
Dry oregano, to taste

SPINACH MIX:
1 lb. fresh spinach, cleaned
2 green onions
Fresh dill and parsley,
*   to taste, finely chopped*
6 tbsp. olive oil
Salt and white pepper, to taste
1/2 lb. Feta cheese, crumbled
2 beaten eggs

4-6 8 oz. fresh chicken breasts
4-6 slices Kasseri cheese (thinly sliced)

Traditional art connects the classic with the contemporary at Pegasus.

Mix the ingredients for the marinade, and marinate the chicken. Put aside.

Mix the ingredients for the spinach mix. Put aside.

In a skillet, sauté the oil, add greens, salt and pepper. Stir and cook about 15 minutes. Remove from heat, and add eggs and Feta. Cool the mixture and let it rest until it reaches room temperature.

Slice the chicken breast open, lengthwise. Take enough spinach mix and fill. Roll the chicken, and fold the sides of the chicken cutlet, envelope style. Repeat with each piece of chicken.

Place in a roasting pan and bake for 15 minutes, at 350 degrees. Remove from the oven and add a thin slice of Kasseri cheese on each roll and sprinkle with paprika for color.

Bake for an additional 15 minutes, until golden brown. Serve warm in whole pieces or sliced.

SERVES 4-6

PASTA WITH VEGETABLES "MAKARONADA AGROTIKI"

This recipe comes from Patras, Greece, with influences from the Ionian island of Corfu. It is a contentious balance of a pasta called hilopites (makaronada) and the harvest of the farmer's (agros) vegetables.

INGREDIENTS
SAUCE:
1/2 lb. unsalted butter
6-8 garlic cloves, thinly sliced
1 fennel bulb, thinly sliced
1 white onion, thinly sliced
1/2 pint heavy cream
Chicken stock liquid

MAKARONADA:
2 lbs. hilopites
1 tbsp. sea salt
1 tbsp. olive oil

VEGETABLES:
1/2 cup olive oil
1/2 lb. white mushrooms, sliced
1/2 lb. broccoli
a handful of sun-dried tomatoes
6-8 fresh artichokes, cleaned
Myzithra cheese to sprinkle
on finished dish

Artopolis Café is a combination bakery, café, bar, gift shop, and coffee house, which serves as a regular meeting place for both young and old. It's a place like no other.

To prepare the sauce, melt the butter in a saucepan, and then add garlic, onions, and fennel. Add white pepper to taste. Mix in stock, lower the heat and let it simmer until liquid is evaporated, about 60 minutes. Turn off the heat and stir in the heavy cream, until sauce thickens.

Prepare the makaronada, by bringing 5-6 cups of water to a boil, in a large pot. Add sea salt to taste, and oil. Add hilopites and boil 5-8 minutes, until al dente. Drain the pasta, and rest on the side of the stove.

For the vegetables, pour oil into a pot. Stir in mushrooms, broccoli, sun-dried tomatoes, and artichokes. Cover and simmer until all water from the vegetables evaporates. Add the cooked pasta, and on a low heat, stir in the sauce. Mix well.

Serve in a pasta dish and sprinkle with Myzithra cheese.

SERVES 6-8

ARTOPITA

*Artopita is the signature creation of Artopolis Bakery and Café. The creation of this tradition-
al form of spanakopita originates from the old world neighborhood bakeries. It's a custom we
faithfully continue. Artopita is made with flaky dough we prepare by hand, and fill with the
freshest selection of herbs and vegetables, fresh from the garden, then bake in our hearth oven.*

INGREDIENTS

*1 lb. fresh spinach leaves,
    fresh or frozen (thawed)*
1/2 of a leek root
*1 white and 1 green onion
    chopped thinly*
Salt and pepper, to taste
2 oz. heavy cream
1 egg beaten
1/2 lb. of Feta cheese

DOUGH MIX:

1 lb. Harvest flour
*4 oz. of prozymi (cultured starter
    dough) or 2 envelopes active
    dry yeast*
2 cups lukewarm water
1 tsp. salt
*2 lbs. unsalted Pulgra (French high-
    fat butter) or regular unsalted
    butter*

This recipe is a condensed version of our famous Artopita,
which makes for easier home preparation.

Combine all ingredients for dough. Knead slightly and
set aside.

If using frozen spinach, thaw, drain, then slice thinly. If using
fresh, wash, drain, and slice thinly. In a frying pan, sauté onions,
leek, and spinach. Remove from heat and let the mix cool. Mix
in heavy cream, egg and Feta, and combine well.

Preheat oven to 350 degrees.

Roll out pastry dough into 2 sheets, approximately 1/4-inch
thick. Be sure to save some dough as a starter for your next
batch of Artopita! Take a shallow, ovenproof glass pie plate and
brush with oil. Place one sheet of dough into the bottom, cover-
ing all sides. Pour in the filling. Cover with the other sheet of
dough and tuck in any edges that fall over the sides of the pan.
Bake for 30-45 minutes, or until golden brown.

SERVES 2-4, depending on size of piece.

PAN FRIED SKATE WING "RANTZA TIGANITI"

Skate wing fish is undeniably one of the best catches in the Mediterranean. This simple recipe comes from Yiayia Calliope and orginates from the island of Lesbos, also known as Mytilene. Rantza Tiganiti, pan fried skate wing, is a tasty dish made from the original recipe of the owner's grandmother.

INGREDIENTS
4-6 Skate wing fillets
Sea salt and white pepper, to taste
Flour
1/2 cup olive oil
Ladolemono (olive oil/lemon juice mixture)
Capers

Wash and rinse fish in cold water. Season with white pepper, sea salt, and then dip in flour to bread.

Warm a heavy skillet, and add 1/2 cup olive oil. Place fish slowly in the pan. Fry until golden on both sides. Remove to a serving plate.

Drizzle on ladolemono, and sprinkle with capers. Serve hot. Serve with whipped or roasted potatoes.

SERVES 4-6

ROAST LEG OF LAMB "ARNI TOU FOURNOU"

This classic recipe was passed on from Yiayia Eugenia, with a strong emphasis on meat preparation and baking perfection. For best results, use fresh herbs and extra virgin olive oil.

INGREDIENTS
1 6-to 8-lb. leg of young spring lamb
6-8 whole garlic cloves
1/2 cup fresh lemon juice
1/2 cup olive oil
1/2 cup hard cheese (optional)
2 cups stock or warm water
Salt and pepper, to taste
Dry oregano, thyme, and rosemary

Wash the lamb. With a sharp knife, make slits in various places on all sides. Inside the slits, insert the garlic cloves and cheese. Season with salt, pepper, oregano, thyme, and rosemary, to taste. Brush with 1/4 cup of olive oil.

Place the lamb in a roasting pan and let it rest 2-3 hours. Preheat the oven to 400 degrees. Sprinkle remaining seasonings on lamb, as well as lemon juice, oil, and the water or stock.

Reduce the oven temperature to 350 degrees, and roast lamb for about 2 hours, turning and basting occasionally.

Slice the meat and serve, surrounded by potatoes or fasolakia (green beans). If desired, potatoes can be roasted in the pan with the lamb. Use 20 small potatoes, peeled and sliced lengthwise.

SERVES 6

HALSTED TODAY

As the residents of Greektown relocated throughout Chicagoland, the effervescent Greek neighborhood dwindled to a few restaurants and businesses, just north on Halsted Street. Andrew A. Athens, National Chairman of the United Hellenic American Congress, along with James Regas, was determined to revive Greektown. Along with local business leaders, they set forth a revitalization and redevelopment plan that would encompass all facets of Greek life and culture and include a national Hellenic Museum and Cultural Center. The project, one of many throughout Chicago, is part of the movement by Mayor Richard M. Daley to rejuvenate the city. The $5 million Greektown project included the erection of two mini-Greek temples to bracket this strip of Halsted Street; as well as three 45-foot tall-sculpted limestone pillars, constructed along the expressway, with each pillar representing a different age of civilization. The rejuvenation also featured streetscape improvements, such as tree planting, the installation of additional lighting, and the rehabilitation of the facades of existing buildings. More importantly, it included the develop-

A Greek-inspired monument welcomes visitors at the north end of Greektown, at the southeast corner of Monroe and Halsted streets.

From the south end of Greektown, looking northwest on to Halsted Street, taken from the future home of the Hellenic Museum and Cultural Center, at 333 South Halsted Street.

ment of a Greek cultural center and museum that would serve as the nucleus of the community, to preserve and perpetuate the Hellenic culture. The redevelopment to initiate these improvements commenced in 1996. By the fall of 2005, the final piece of the puzzle began to fall in place, with the demolition of the existing building at 333 South Halsted – the site of the new

A replica of a Greek temple and a statue of Athena, Goddess of Wisdom, welcome visitors at the south end of Greektown, at the southeast corner of Halsted and Van Buren streets.

The Goddess Athena presented the olive tree to the Greeks, and for this treasured gift the city of Athens was named for her. She is said to protect and watch over her namesake city, and with this statue, she protects and watches over Greektown as well.

Hellenic Museum and Cultural Center.

Halsted today is alive and thriving. It's a place where Greeks and people from all walks of life converge for a slice of Greek culture. In Greektown, one may sample Greek cuisine, purchase Greek pastries, music, video, gifts, religious items, and, of course, dance until dawn. The surrounding neighborhood is being redeveloped into a residential area, and Greektown today is, indeed, a vibrant and flourishing Chicago neighborhood.

The Chicago Skyline shimmers at night looking east from Halsted Street with the Sears Tower, once the tallest building in the world, standing proud in the center. Greektown comes alive at night. Restaurants and dance clubs welcome visitors from diverse ethnic groups, from all over the world.

"I always enjoyed Greektown for the food. My favorite restaurant there is Rodity's. I remember one time we went to the White Sox game and afterwards we went there for dinner, and one of my friends who was not Greek insisted that he didn't need help on the menu. So, when the waiter came over to him, he was mulling over the menu and he had that gleam in his eye like he found what he wanted and he looked at the waiter and said, 'I'm going to have some of that pistachio!' What he was trying to say was 'pastitsio.' We laughed our heads off!"

Greektown is not only easily accessible from downtown and the suburbs, but also has ample parking. Valets greet customers outside restaurants for
curbside service. For those who prefer not to valet,
there are many parking lots on Halsted, as well as
around the corner to the west, on Green Street.
Unlike many downtown areas, Greektown
parking is plentiful and inexpensive.

"Greece is lovely. No question about
it. But, there is something about
Chicago that is even better. You
have everything at your fingertips."

Greek Americans poured onto Halsted Street to celebrate Greece's Euro Cup championship victory, defeating Portugal 1-0 in July 2004. People danced in the street and proudly waved their Greek flags, shouting "Zito Ellada!" meaning, "Long live Greece!"

Andrew A. Athens, president of the United Hellenic American Congress (UHAC), as well as the president of the World Council of Hellenes Abroad (SAE), was instrumental in spearheading Greektown's restoration in the mid-1990s. Here, he addresses the community at a special groundbreaking ceremony, in 1996, attended by guests, left to right: His Eminence Metropolitan Iakovos of Krinis, presiding Hierarch of Chicago; James Regas, Project Coordinator; Chris Tomaras, vice president of SAE America; former President of the Republic of Greece, Costis Stephanopoulos, with sunglasses. Not pictured is special guest Chicago Mayor Richard M. Daley.

Chicago has several resident Greek dance troupes, including the Olympian Greek Dance Troupe who has entertained audiences since 1988. The troupe poses in front of the Cloud Gate sculpture, fondly known as the "Bean" at Chicago's new Millennium Park. The Olympians, as well as other dance troupes, perform at cultural events throughout Chicagoland.

Greek influence can be seen in buildings and statues throughout Chicago. Architects continue to use Greek columns of every style, to lend classic authority to numerous financial institutions, government buildings, as well as art centers. Some Chicago examples include the Doric columns at Soldier Field, the Ionic columns gracing the entryway to the Field Museum, and the Corinthian columns used to frame the entryway to the old London Guarantee and Occidental Building on Michigan Avenue. Pictured is a Greek-inspired monument that adorns the entrance to Millennium Park.

Greektown restaurants and merchants participate in the annual "Taste of Greece." At the end of August since the late 1990s, Halsted Street has been closed from Monroe to Van Buren, for a street festival celebrating all things Greek. People from all walks of life, throughout the city and suburbs, converge on Halsted to partake in a slice of Greek culture. Festivalgoers celebrate the joys of Hellenism, through the culinary delights of Greektown, combined with live Greek music and dancing, and of course, a good bottle of wine.

Confectionery artifacts from Dove Candies, Cupid Candies, and Chicago Candy Company.

Embroidered textile, created by Kalliope Smirniotis.

HELLENIC MUSEUM AND CULTURAL CENTER

A Quiet Odyssey Emerges in Chicago's Historic Greektown Neighborhood

Where might one go to learn about the Greek immigrant experience in America, view vignettes from a permanent collection of over 6,000 objects, photos, century-old books, film, 18th and 19th century textiles, even Cypriot antiquities?

Imagine a place where generations at a time walk into a gallery to hear the recordings and visual testimonials that capture "Growing up Greek in America," living through homeland wars and famine or the joy of experiencing a new generation of success.

This is a glimpse of a visitor's experience at the national Hellenic Museum and Cultural Center.

For many years, members of our Greek-American community talked about the desirability of having a Hellenic Museum to preserve our heritage. In 1982, the Hellenic Museum and Cultural Center, a National Institution, was formally established.

In the years that followed, Alec and Viena K. Gianaras, who believed that such a Museum should become a reality, made a gift of $100,000 to begin the work. This enabled the newly formed Museum board to hold an inaugural exhibit, "Celebrating Hellenism" in May 1992. The exhibit included 18th century Byzantine art and embroideries from the 18th century, contemporary art from noted Chicago artists, and family treasures preserved by Greek immigrants.

Following this exhibit, the Museum collected archival materials, established a library, offered workshops in Greek folk arts, mounted new exhibits, and showcased works of Greek and Greek-American artists, promising musicians, educators, and scholars.

When the original building at 400 North Franklin was sold, the facility moved to the then National Bank of Greece building at 168 North Michigan until November 2003 when it moved to 801 West Adams Street in Chicago's Greektown. This temporary facility occupies approximately 10,000 square feet of space over the Greek Islands building.

Furthermore, by 2008, the Hellenic Museum is expected to complete the nation's first 40,000 square-foot facility devoted to Greek culture. The building will be located on the corner of Halsted and Van Buren streets in the heart of Chicago's Greektown neighborhood. Its mission is to be the nation's foremost center of Hellenic history, culture, and the arts, where the public can explore the legacy of the Greek immigrant experience in America and examine the influence of Hellenic culture and peoples from antiquity to the present.

Traditional wedding dress from the village of Hlomp, Epirus, circa 1924.

Cypriot antiquities, circa 800-700 B.C.

CONTRIBUTORS

Helen Alexander
George Alposianis
James Apostolopoulos
Sophie R. Andrikopoulos
Andrew Athens
Ulysses Paul Backas
George Bacos
Don Benz
Angeline Boosalis
Kenny Brejcha
Antonia Callas
Nick Callas
Dr. Elaine Pierce Chakonas
Costa Caris
Constance Constant
Fr. Evagoras Constantinides
Maria Constantinides
Jim Contis
Kosta Dalageorgas
Rose and George Dalianis
Phillip DeFrancisco
Thula DeMets
Gene Douglas
Elaine Kollintzas Drikakis
Alice Ducas
Rose Economou
Panos and Irene Fiorentinos
Maria Fotinopoulos
Steve Frangos
Ada and Richard Frank
Sandra Ganakos
Effie Gekas
Christine George
Chris Georges
Helen Georges

Harry Gio
Anna Greanias-Wright
Greek Star Newspaper
Hellenic Museum and
    Cultural Center
Allison Heller Fluecke
Christina Hiotis
Christina Sofiakis-Hoidas
James Kacheres
William and Mary Kakavas
Tess Kakis
Christina Kanatas
The Very Rev. Archimandrite
    Demetri Kantzavelos
Bertha Kartinos
Constantine Katsaros
Elaine and Lou Katzioris
Diane Kavelaras
Andrew and Alice Kopan
Petros Kogiones
Bessie Kouchoukos-Grosso
Lalagos Family
Antigonie Lambros
Fay Machinis
Erin McCarthy
Louis and Helen Malevitis
Louis and Carol Mallers
Natonia Malleris
Angie Malouhos
Cleo and Samuel Maragos
Helen Marlas
Deanne Mavrick
James M. Mezilson
Georgia Mitchell
Ernie Neokos

Olympian Dance Troupe
Orpheus Hellenic Folklore
    Society
Adrienne Papadakos
Jean Paspalas
Angela Gregory Paterakis
Despina H. Paulson
Angelo Pavlatos
Olga Paxinos
Harold and Faye Peponis
Harry Mark Petrakis
James and Penny Petropoul
Elaine Harris Rathjen
Renee Scheider
Rima Lunin Schultz
John H. Secaras
Magda Simopoulos
Mariana Spyropoulos
Ted Spyropoulos
Hon. John J. Stamos
Joanne Stavrakas
Kathy Stratton
Mike Stefanos
Ann Stevens
Andrew Stotts
Jane Terovolas
Crystella Terevolos
Elaine Thomopoulos
Themis and Frances Tsaussis
Themi Vasils
Theana Vavasis
Stephanie Vlahakis
Mike Vlamis
Janine Weiss

PHOTO CREDITS

We would like to thank the following public and commercial contributors for providing photographs used in this book. Many of the images used were from private collections and we would like to express our appreciation to them as well. We would be poorly served and informed without the worthwhile efforts of these groups to preserve and record the images and history of the Greek community.

Abraham Lincoln Presidential
    Library, Springfield, Illinois;
    pages 16, 17, 28-R, 29-L.
Andrew Stotts; page 194.
Chicago Historical Society, Chicago,
    Illinois; pages 14, 35.
GreekCircle Magazine; numerous
    images.
The Greek Star newspaper; various
    images.
Hellenic Museum and Cultural
    Center, Chicago, Illinois;
    numerous images.
Jessica Tampas; author photo
Panos Fiorentinos; pages 128-R, 129-BL,
    129-TR, 130-ML, 130-BL, 132-TR.
The University of Illinois at Chicago,
    The University Library, Jane
    Addams Memorial Collection,
    Daley Library Special Collections
    Department, Chicago, Illinois;
    pages 14, 15-BL, 15-M, 19, 20, 19-
    TR, 22-TL, 23-TR, 24-BL, 24-BR,
    25-T, 25-B, 29-R, 30-L, 30-R, 39.

ACKNOWLEDGEMENTS

Photography has always been a passion of mine, and to have this opportunity to create a history and recipe book celebrating the spirit of Greeks in Chicago using both pictures and words, has been a cherished moment in my life. Because of the strong pride shown in being Greek American, I am thankful for the outpouring of support by the Chicago Greek community who opened their hearts and homes to create this book. From the photos, recipes, and collection of quotations–the community has embraced this project to help create a keepsake of our Greek heritage.

I'd like to give special thanks to the Hellenic Museum and Cultural Center staff who guided me through the museum's archival collections. And, especially to the Oral History Committee and Columbia College, whose students conducted many of the oral histories that were excerpted throughout the book and helped to give a first-person account of the immigration and daily living experiences of Greek Americans.

On the production side, thank you to Brad Baraks and his staff whose expertise in publishing helped to provide an exquisite memory book giving Greeks the recognition they deserve for their contributions to Chicago and to the United States. And, to the talented Katherine Bish, whose warm personality radiated through her photography within the homes and restaurants featured in this book.

I would like to give my deepest appreciation to my family, Gregory, Sandra, Stephanie, and Melissa, who have always supported my endeavors with patience, love, and enthusiasm, as well as to the energetic staff and editorial contributors of *GreekCircle* magazine. Last, but not least, I'd like to thank Christopher, who stepped into my life outside of a Greektown restaurant on the famed Halsted Street featured in this book. He has shown me love, respect, and encouragement and has helped to make celebrating my Greek heritage even more special.

BIBLIOGRAPHY

Abbott, Grace, "A Study of the Greeks in Chicago," *The American Journal of Sociology*, November 10, 1909.

Crawford, Gary, "National Hellenic Invitational Basketball Tournament," *GreekCircle*, Spring 2004.

Constant, Constance M., *Austin Lunch: Greek American Recollections*, Cosmos Publishing, 2005.

Coulolias, Vikki, "Greek Festivals: A Summer Tradition," *GreekCircle*, Spring 2002.

Demas, Lane, "Immigrant Entrepreneurs and the Formation of Chicago's Greektown (1890-1921)," Illinois Historic Preservation Conference, University of California at Irvine, October 9, 2003.

Diacou, Stacy, *Hellenism in Chicago*, United Hellenic American Congress, 1982.

Fiorentinos, Panos, *Ecclesia: Greek Orthodox Churches of the Chicago Metropolis*, Kantyli Inc., 2004. www.greekchurchbook.com

Fotinopoulos, Maria, "The Joy of Chocolate," *GreekCircle*, Winter 2004.

Frangos, Steve A., "Greektown Reunion," *The Greek Star*, 2002.

Hull House Bulletin, 1896-1906.

Ingram, Scott, "Immigration to the United States: Greek Immigrants," Facts on File, Inc. 2005.

Kopan, Andrew T. Ph.D., *Greek Survival in Chicago, Ethnic Chicago*, William B. Eerdmans Publishing, 1995.

Lissner, Connie, "The Coffee Shop as Comfort Food," Winter 2002, and "All in the Family," Summer 2002 *GreekCircle*.

Peterson, Tiffany, *Greek Americans*, Heinemann Library, 2004.

Scourby, Alice, *The Greek Americans*, Twayne Publishers, 1984.

Thomopoulos, Ph.D., Elaine Cotsirilos; Kopan, Ph.D., Andrew T.; Kopan, M.A., M.Ed., Alice Orphanos; Kallen, Vivian Margaris; Ashford, Ph.D., J.D., Nicholas Askounes, *Images of America: Greek-American Pioneer Women of Illinois*, the Greek Women's University Club, Arcadia Publishing, 2000.

Tzakis, Dimitria, "The Hellenic Debutante Cotillion: A Historical Overview," *GreekCircle*, Winter 2002.

Walker, Natalie, "Greeks and Italians in the Neighborhood of Hull House," *The American Journal of Sociology*, Volume XXI, No. 3, November 1915.

Zurales, Toni, "OPA! Greek Dancing, The Music of Life," Fall 2001 and "Sweet Success," Summer 2002, *GreekCircle* .

EPILOGUE

In looking back, we can certainly see that times have changed. From their first steps on the shores of America as immigrants, Greek Americans have risen to positions of leadership in business and in the community. They took it upon themselves to establish churches, organizations, nursing and retirement centers, museums, and schools to keep alive the Greek cultural heritage. And, the bond created through these entities is one of the reasons the Greek American community has remained united in spirit, if not in location.

When the central old Greektown neighborhood was lost to urban expansion, the Greeks moved throughout the city and suburbs. They planted their strong Greek roots whereever they moved and contributed to the heart and soul of Chicagoland. Even though the Greeks were once displaced to make room for expressways and a college campus, there was a small twist of fate that allowed them to continue to have a strong underlying presence in the area, other than just the lively shops and restaurants that line the present-day Halsted Street. Greek Americans continue to make up a significant part of the old Greektown neighborhood through their attendance at the University of Illinois at Chicago, boasting the highest attendance of Greek Americans of any university in the state. And the Modern Greek Studies Program was recently established there through the Foundation for Hellenic Studies.

In addition, the promise of a new, state-of-the-art facility, and continued quality exhibitions organized by the Hellenic Museum and Cultural Center, serve as programs that signify a rebirth of the Greektown area and continue to educate and enrich us as proud Greek Americans.

If a picture is worth a thousand words, then the truest history lies in photography where those fragile emulsions, unedited and unabridged, capture the true past. It is hoped that this keepsake book of photos, food, and history serves as a remembrance of our collective accomplishments as Greek Americans, and gives us the momentum to continue the preservation of our rich past for future generations.

FOOTNOTES

1. "On the changing neighborhood and the dramatic sudden appearance, early in the century, of a large colony of Greeks." *Eighty Years at Hull House*, Edited by Allen F. Davis and Mary Lynn McCree, 1969

2. "A Study of the Greeks in Chicago" by Grace Abbott, *The American Journal of Sociology*, Vol XV, No. 3, November 1909

3. Georgia Veremis, in an interview by Mary Ann Johnson, 4/14/78, Hull-House Oral History Collection, OH-046, Special Collections, University Library, University of Illinois at Chicago

4. *Hull House Year Book*, September 1, 1906-1907

5. *1960: Jane Addams Centennial* by D. Michalaros, Athene, Autumn 1960

6. *Hull House Year Book*, January 1, 1913

7. Judge James Zafiratos, in an interview by Beth Bailey, 8/22/84, Hull-House Oral History Collection, OH-050, Special Collections, University Library, University of Illinois at Chicago

8. "Greek Survival in Chicago," *Ethnic Chicago*, Andrew Kopan, Eerdmans Publishing, 2005.

9. Mr. Lorado Taft on the Greek play *Odysseus*, Hull House Bulletin, Vol. IV, No.1, 1900

10. *Hull House Year Book*, 1929

11. Francis Hackett, an Irish immigrant who came to live at Hull House in 1906 when he was 23 years old. He was an editorial writer for the *Chicago Evening Post* and wrote *Hull House – A Souvenir* (1925)

12. *Goodbye Greektown* by Constantine D. Orphan, *Inland, The Magazine of the Middlewest*, Spring 1963

13. *Eighty Years at Hull House*, Edited by Allen F. Davis and Mary Lynn McCree, 1969

14. "A Study of the Greeks in Chicago," pp. 380-381, *The American Journal of Sociology*, Grace Abbott, Director of the Immigrant Protective League, November 1909

14.5. Frangos, Steve A., "The History of Halsted," *GreekCircle*, Fall 2002

15. Hull House Bulletin, Vol. VII. No. 1, 1905-1906

16. *A Study of the Greeks in Chicago* by Grace Abbott, *The American Journal of Sociology*, Vol XV, No. 3, November 1909

17. *Goodbye Greektown* by Constantine D. Orphan, *Inland, The Magazine of the Middlewest*, Spring 1963

18. "Wide Interest Shown in Revival of Greek Club" by Donna Hodgman, Hull House Block News, Friday, January 27, 1939, Vol. II, No. 7

19. on The Acropolis Restaurant and Tavern at 646-9 Blue Island Avenue, owned by James Lalagos